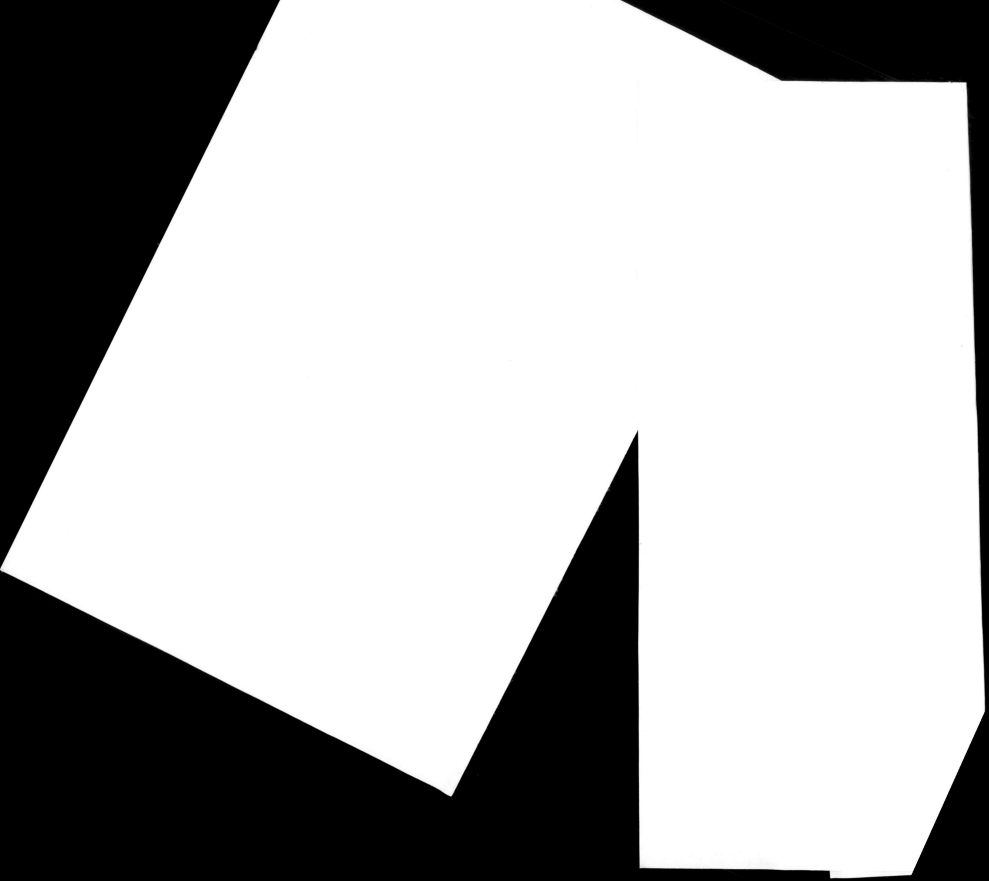

# RUDE DEMOCRACY

## Civility and Incivility in American Politics

SUSAN HERBST

TEMPLE UNIVERSITY PRESS  PHILADELPHIA

TEMPLE UNIVERSITY PRESS
Philadelphia, Pennsylvania 19122
www.temple.edu/tempress

Copyright © 2010 by Temple University
All rights reserved
Published 2010

Library of Congress Cataloging-in-Publication Data
Herbst, Susan.
 Rude democracy: civility and incivility in American politics / Susan Herbst.
  p. cm.
 Includes bibliographical references and index.
 ISBN 978-1-4399-0335-3 (cloth: alk. paper) — ISBN 978-1-4399-0337-7 (electronic)
 1. Courtesy—Political aspects—United States. 2. Political culture—United States.
 3. United States—Politics and government—2009– I. Title.
 JK1726.H47 2010
 306.20973—dc22
                                                              2010010586

∞ The paper used in this publication meets the requirements of the American National
Standard for Information Sciences—Permanence of Paper for Printed Library Materials,
ANSI Z39.48-1992

Printed in the United States of America

2  4  6  8  9  7  5  3  1

*In memory of my father,*

*Adolph Herbst:*

*Ideal-typical democratic citizen*

# Contents

# Acknowledgments

I t was challenging for me, a social scientist with a historical bent, to write a book on contemporary American political culture. We witness dramatic change with every passing month—more partisan bickering than we believed possible, an evolving Internet that shapes journalistic practice, and a shifting international scene that has most citizens anxious with concern. When this book is distributed, we shall no doubt be in a somewhat different context than we are today. But I hope that, as we navigate these early decades of the twenty-first century, I have at least opened new avenues for discussion and study.

As historians know, our current period is not the first time we have seen incivility, name-calling, and brutal rhetoric in politics. The cover of this book—the famous 1856 attack on Senator Charles Sumner by Congressman Preston Brooks on the floor of the U.S. Senate—illustrates our long struggle with incivility. These were dark days for a nation on the brink of civil war, fighting an emotional battle over slavery that none of us today can possibly fathom. And some will recall that Franklin Roosevelt's New Deal policies were met with harsh rhetoric in the following century—including claims that the president was a fascist and a communist. Understanding these historical swells of name-calling and intense anger may not make incivility easier to stomach, but it does put today's horrors of public discourse into a context important for all Americans to understand.

I wrote this book as a professor but also as an administrator with the University System of Georgia, and I am grateful to my terrific colleagues, who encourage research and scholarship daily. Tom Daniel, Tim Hynes, and the extraordinarily wise Regent Willis Potts of Rome, Georgia, read the entire manuscript and supported the project with vigor. Our former Board Chair, Richard Tucker, was an incisive and steadfast supporter. It has been my great honor to serve on the faculty at the Georgia Institute of Technology, and I thank my students for setting me straight many times: They give me hope that our young people will create a far better, more civil, and more humane American politics. At Georgia Tech, Richard Barke, Diana Hicks, Sue Rosser (now provost at San Francisco State), Gary Schuster, Dene Sheheane, and our stellar president, Bud Peterson, have made my every moment on campus a real pleasure. James Bason, director of the UGA Survey Research Center, was critical to the data collection in Chapter 5.

Alex Holzman, director of Temple University Press, has been my editor and my friend for fifteen years, and I could not be more grateful for his support and wisdom. John Geer of Vanderbilt University and Kevin Barnhurst of the University of Illinois gave me some terrific criticism, and I greatly value their keen scholarly judgment. Mendi Spencer has been my best colleague for a long while. I cannot thank her enough for support and counsel on a daily basis.

The enduring love and hilarity of our household—led by my husband, Doug, and my children, Daniel and Rebecca—may not always be a model of civility, but we like it just fine, and it is the foundation for all I am. Finally, this book is dedicated to the memory of my father, holocaust survivor and once stateless person, who lived the ideals of American civility without ever having to think about it.

# RUDE DEMOCRACY

# 1 / The Powerful—if Elusive—
# Nature of Civility

Give me thy hand: I am sorry I beat thee; but, while
thou livest, keep a good tongue in thy head.

STEPHANO, in Shakespeare's *The Tempest*, ACT III

Many senators said the current vitriol [over health care
legislation] . . . was unlike anything they had seen.
"It has gotten so much more partisan," said Senator
John D. Rockefeller IV, Democrat of West Virginia.
"This was so wicked. This was so venal."

DAVID HERSZENHORN,
"In Health Vote, A New Vitriol," *New York Times*

High-minded rhetoric about "civility" courses throughout issue debates across the nation. We find hopes for civility expressed in speeches by the mighty all the way down to the posts of lone, unknown bloggers. But the gap between our language about civility and the real nature of American political discourse and practice is at least as wide as it has ever been. This book explores that gap—what it looks like, how it persists, and whether it matters for a contemporary democracy like our own.

Our particular historical moment is fraught with the concerns of our day: an economic downturn, energy independence, health care reform, the conduct of major military efforts in Afghanistan and Iraq, and a fierce ideological divide between political parties that seems to grow worse each month. It is also a moment created—most of all, perhaps—by the extraordinary presidential campaigns of 2008, and an equally extraordinary election outcome. Presidential elections and their aftermaths, despite their uniqueness, have proven to be among the best analytic tools we have for studying our political culture, and they are superb windows into the nature of civility. So my focus in this book is on civility writ large in American politics, but viewed through the distinctive lens of the 2008 campaigns and election.

Because the debates about health care reform have continued to evolve, I have been able extend my analysis well into the winter of 2010, even though this national discussion remained far from settled. Some town hall meetings, called to debate health care reform in the summer of 2009, challenged many ideals about civility. And the now infamous shout "You lie!"—uttered by South Carolina's Representative Joe Wilson during President Barack Obama's address to a joint session of Congress in September 2009—marked some sort of American milestone. But in many ways the passionate absence of bipartisanship and the accolades Wilson gathered from his party reflect an anger that had developed during the 2008 presidential election campaign. Fallout from that election and new manifestations of party conflict have much to do with civility.[1]

It was unexpected, but our most recent presidential contest turned out to be particularly helpful in studying the contemporary practice of both civility and incivility. It boasted a variety of fascinating aspects—the tenor of the campaigns, the tone and content of media coverage, and the nature of interpersonal dialogues all around us. While voter turnout figures may have been a disappointment to scholars hoping for astronomical numbers, there is no question that—although impossible to measure precisely—emotions ran much higher than those from prior recent presidential elections. We might speculate on why the emotional pitch was so high. An economic downturn of epic proportions? The first African American presidential candidate? The proliferation of engaging Web sites and bloggers? Fierce, lengthy primary battles? No matter the causes, it was a riveting year of campaigns, and we are forever changed by the people and events of 2008.

It seems clear in retrospect that 2008 mattered to Americans in profound ways. In a context where an already-intense campaign was ratcheted up by a severe recession and two wars in progress, civility was bound to emerge as a central issue. Was the campaign civil, or should we say, civil enough for America? Did those who participated in it—from candidates to journalists to citizens—treat each other with the respect deemed appropriate in our (self-proclaimed) world's greatest democracy? And, most interesting, should we even worry about civility, a "pie-in-the-sky" concept with an old-fashioned, nine-teenth-century ring to it?

When I told people I was writing a book on civility, they thought of opening doors for women, naughty children misbehaving in pub-lic, and suppressing the desire to give others "the finger" in traffic. These niceties or hoped-for niceties are related to civility, no doubt. But my interest is in the fundamental tone and practice of democ-racy, in the wake of an unusual presidential campaign and at the start of the twenty-first century.

While a single presidential election offers but one window into the debates over civility, my empirical investigations seem to point to far larger, longitudinal conundrums of political culture. Some Amer-icans, citizens and leaders, are distraught about what they see as a decline in civility. Others find the worriers both naïve and cowardly: The line between passionate engagement and civility seems chroni-cally fuzzy and arbitrary. Both views can be persuasive, and it does us no good to choose sides. Norms of civility certainly exist, as we shall see throughout this book. But civility is also very much in the eye of the beholder. Where you sit—as a journalist, an ideologue, a candi-date, or a citizen—matters immensely. Perspectives vary, and while this is all somewhat messy, it suits a democracy that must wrestle with both policy and the tone of policy debate.

The questions I want to raise about civility are challenging to answer, and the vague meaning of "civility" has much to do with that challenge. But as I argue in this book, debates over its definition, its rise, or its fall are a distraction. What we should attend to are the

*Perhaps a as a definition of useful discourse and the exchange of ideas*

*strategic uses* of civility and incivility. Civility is best thought of as an asset or tool, a mechanism, or even a technology of sorts. As I explain in this chapter, this approach opens up a wide and productive range of empirical phenomena to study *and* captures the context-dependent, historical nature of civility. If we think of civility as a strategic asset, we can pull away from the "more or less" debates and study newer forms of political discourse and behavior with far more sophistication and success.

I assume a strong free-speech framework. There is no question, as we will see in the pages that follow, that much uncivil talk in our present-day political communication is racist, sexist, or just plain rude. No one, except a mindless provocateur, would want these sorts of hateful speech acts to be commonplace. And, of course, speech that threatens violence—as we saw in the aftermath of the March health care bill passage in 2010—is unacceptable. But in my work, I have come to admit that lines are fuzzy and that *imputation* of motives from rhetoric is a dangerous game. Congressman Joe Wilson's 2009 shout at President Obama provoked considerable debate about underlying racial motives: Would he have yelled at a white president? Why the shout during Obama's discussion of illegal immigrants? I'm afraid that answers to such questions are elusive, empirically at least, regardless of our gut feeling. So while I do indeed find certain remarks clearly inappropriate, I will hold judgment on what I think is and is not constructive debate. I leave these matters to editorial writers and thinkers who seek particular policy or social change. They are important matters, but are not the topic of this book.

Another assumption I make here is that "facts"—notions that we can prove through widely accepted standards of evidence—are important in democratic debate, but they may have only a marginal relationship to the struggle over civility. Of course, facts matter, and there is tremendous interest in them, hence the appearance of "fact-checking" Web sites that put our political officials under scrutiny. This is absolutely essential work in any polity, without question. But there are significant gray areas, both during political campaigns and between them, so again, I tread carefully. When leaders are actively, intentionally deceiving us, and we can prove—perhaps at a much later date—that they knew they lied, where do we place this phenomenon in relation to civility?

My belief is that truly interesting and important cases of intentional public lying are somewhat rare, and that creative stretching of the truths one holds dear is probably far more common. In any case, awful lies are typically revealed after the debate in question has passed, and they should be judged with vigor whenever they appear. The challenge of determining who is using facts well and who is not is a moving target, and I applaud the effort, even if it is a rough fit to thinking about civility.[2]

## Three Arguments about Civility

My central argument concerns the strategic natures of civility and incivility—as employed in blogs, in speeches, at campaign rallies, and in face-to-face discussions. But I posit two additional arguments, aspects of civility beyond strategy.

First, in our quest for political discussion and interchange, we have come to need a fair amount of comfort and interactivity. The "Oprah-like" culture of therapy—feeling good about our human interactions, or at least not feeling bad—has led us to avoid, or be disturbed by, even minor feelings of discomfort in political discourse, whether televised, on the Web, or in person. In addition (sometimes in tension with the need for comfort, sometimes not), our generalized desire for interaction and reciprocity is vital to how we see civility. This is likely an effect of the Internet, with its constant presence in our lives, and the feedback it so often provides. (Chapter 5 addresses the Internet.)

Civility is a complex notion, and my three conceptual approaches emerge from past literature and current practice, viewed at least partially through the particular lens of 2008. Focusing on *strategic* civility provides a way to analyze our political environment effectively and, at the same time, avoid inconclusive debates about whether civility is on the rise or decline. The other two arguments concern the nature of the civility that we seem to desire as Americans: Civility has both *emotional* and *interactive* components that are limiting but important, as we parse contemporary American politics.

## Strategic Civility

It is most useful to think of civility as a tool in the rhetorical and behavioral arsenals of politics.[3] Sometimes people are unknowingly civil or uncivil, of course. These actions may be natural aspects of our typical participation in politics. Indeed, some individuals seem to emanate civility or incivility as part of their approach, so much so that it seems central to their very fabric of being. While partisanship abounds in the higher reaches of American politics, it is fair to say, for example, that a variety of U.S. senators, past and present, have been consistently civil in their behavior. This is one reason why they are commonly selected for sensitive and controversial tasks. (For example, Senator George Mitchell was chosen to investigate illegal uses of performance-enhancing drugs in baseball, and then was chosen as Middle East envoy.) And on the uncivil end of the continuum, we have actors like the late Lee Atwater, a political consultant who broke new ground in the pursuit of brutal and highly personal campaign mudslinging.

Apart from these cases of chronic, uniform, or innate civility or incivility, which are unusual, we should think of civility as a strategic tool or weapon in politics. It is a tool that is used intentionally, for better or worse. Someone might use incivility to great effect in a negative advertising campaign. Or, alternately, take the "high road" in advertising, hoping to gain accolades for the use of civility and even generosity of feeling toward an opponent. As noted previously, many have viewed civility as a state of a society (more or less civil) and a constellation of social norms associated with that state. I differ in this book, treating it is a tool. Table 1.1 sets out characteristics implied by the two different perspectives on civility.

### TABLE 1.1 TWO APPROACHES TO CIVILITY

| Civility as a Set of Norms | Civility as a Strategic Tool |
| --- | --- |
| Static, within eras | Temporary and changeable |
| Conflated with culture | Easily discerned and singled out |
| Tethered to a context | Fluid in use across contexts |
| Without a particular communicator | With a clear communicating agent |
| Not conducive to Internet communication styles | Conducive to Internet communication styles |
| Difficult to manipulate intimacy by communicators | Easy to manipulate intimacy by communicators |

As we shall see in the brief review of civility through the nineteenth and twentieth centuries that follows, most theorists, historians, and writers have viewed civility as a set of social and cultural norms. These observers find different levels of civility in different eras. Some see civility on the rise, and others see it in decline, scholars Stephen Carter and Robert Putnam being among the strongest proponents of the latter view. But if we think of civility as something employed for tactical purposes, we are able to pull away from these debates, which are not always as productive as they might be in an age of Web communication. This is not to say that these scholars have not contributed to the study of civility; they have done so mightily, with erudition and panache. But the time has come to shift the debate and analysis of civility. With the arrival of the Internet, we have a seemingly endless number of communicators, forever inventing new sites, channels, and techniques for persuasion, conversation, and assault.

If, as in Table 1.1, we view civility as most authors have—as a set of norms and practices—we are left with a generally static approach. Of course, the norms and ideas about civility change, but typically such changes take decades and often generations to occur. However, we now live in an intensely communicative age where no one waits on the passage of decades: These days, communicators are utilizing, playing with, and transforming civility and incivility daily, shaping American political discourse as a result.

Sometimes the experimentation of bloggers and average citizens challenges broader cultural norms in profound ways, as we saw during the 2008 presidential election. One particularly interesting example was the role of YouTube: A variety of contributors to the site posted video footage (taken surreptitiously) of people removing Obama or McCain yard signs.[4] This is a superb illustration of the complex uses of incivility, one that would be difficult to parse and understand if we did not think about civility and incivility as weapons. People steal or deface signs in order to further their own candidate in a local community. Then, enterprising people catch thieves on video, thereby exposing the practice but raising the implicit prospect that stealing yard signs has become *normative*—an acceptable ground game of politics.

Again, the older view of civility as a norm (the first column) cannot help us with these new, more complicated activities, made possible by the Internet, viewed by tens of millions. YouTube, as well as many other sites, enables people to make arguments through video, audio, blogging, and chatting. If we see civility as a strategic tool, it becomes a rich, relevant topic again, one that could not be more fitting to an Internet age, with so many varied participants worldwide. The old ways of thinking about civility—as a static part of culture, not easily manipulated or quickly altered, that is widely shared—seem downright inappropriate. These days, civility can be exploited or not, with tremendous speed and ease. Communicators can "grab" it for their purposes, and the venues for the uses of civility and incivility seem limitless. Far beyond stealing or destroying signs, fascinating as that is, are the "photoshopping" of images (e.g., candidate faces attached to other bodies), the continual distortion and reediting of candidate videos, citizen battles via Wikipedia page revisions, the chronic decontextualization of quotations, speeches, and ideas, and a variety of other communicative actions, easy enough for middle school children to carry out.

One question that arises when we treat civility and incivility as strategic tools is whether they are good or bad, helpful or hurtful for democracy. An easy answer is the one we so often see in the scholarly politics literature: Incivility is destructive and blocks proper democratic debate. I find this a banal and unsophisticated answer, one that ignores the reality of politics, communication culture, and the social environment of the twenty-first century. In this book, I do not dodge this question, but there is no definitive answer to it either, and we would be dishonest to grandstand on it. It depends entirely on issue and situational context, and is closely tied to ideology and passion. Someone who believes that an embryo is a human being, for example, thinks it good for democracy and morality to use incivility—perhaps peacefully displaying images of horribly destroyed fetuses—as a strategic weapon. To these actors, such discourse enhances the debate and injects vital reality to it. And there are examples from the political left, just as powerful. In fact, Herbert Marcuse, a leading Marxist public intellectual of the 1960s, advocated forms of incivility—harsh interference with the speech of others, for example—if they furthered the values of social movements and justice.[5] In any case, it is not productive to go round and round on these matters, but better to evaluate them in the context of a national debate, as I do in Chapter 3, when discussing the 2009 health care policy "town meetings." And in my conclusion, I will argue that tying ourselves up in knots about what is right or wrong, civil or uncivil, is far less useful than educating Americans about how to debate and develop the thick skin that strong democratic debate demands. *The real question is whether we want both depth of debate and the work that comes with it.*

Nonetheless, my thesis may be hard to swallow for some, because we have for so long seen the issues as black and white—civility is good, incivility is bad. Would not acceptance of incivility as a valid rhetorical tool like so many others lead to even more tactical, nasty, and ultimately destructive public discourse? Far from it, as I argue throughout this book. If we see civility and incivility as strategic assets, we humanize the players on our political scene, in our town councils, and in our workplaces. Civil people can say uncivil things and uncivil people can be civil. Second, thinking about the *uses* of civility and incivility boosts our self-consciousness about the nature of political talk, reflection that is absolutely essential for a healthy nation. Finally, if we can view uncivil talk as just that, there can be change: If civility and incivility are "states" and not "traits," as the early psychologists used to say, how we talk to each other is changeable—daily.

## Civility, Comfort, and Personalized Interactivity

It has become clear that the nature of civility is conflated with both feeling and interactive discourse in our time. In a culture where emotion is a dominant concept, used to describe everything from workplace dynamics to international diplomacy, we tend to think of civil behavior in the context of how it makes us feel. And we seem to know best how we feel, as a population, through our engagement with media—the nature and content of our "personal" media (our e-mail, our online relationships), as well as more distant media (pundits we watch or blogs we read). To attain "civility" in the twenty-first century, I posit here, is to achieve emotional affirmation *and* to have done so through immediate, intense communication. Put another way, civility is about feeling good while we interact with others, whether in person or through Twitter and Facebook. These dual components of civility—emotional comfort and intimacy in communication—are two broad axes around which my subsequent, more particular arguments revolve.[6]

It is good to feel good, while engaged in any social behavior. But one result of our current mode of civility is the anxiety produced by uncomfortable political interaction. Are we truly open to heated debate? What happens when we head toward the more intensive, passionately ideological, or even cruel exchange of words? Does a "take-no-prisoners" form of debate or journalism have a place in our current culture of civility? These are questions I take up later, and they are central to understanding our own moment in politics.

How we treat each other in democracy has long been the realm of political philosophers and more recently cultural historians as well. The nature of our "manners," often conflated with civility, has also been of great interest to scholars and writers for centuries. But there is no question that changes in media infrastructure, the rise of the Internet, and our seemingly endless need to take our personal and collective emotional temperatures demand that we evaluate civility and its future in new ways. Throughout this book, in trying to understand what civility is and should be, I will come back to the themes of feeling and communication, in hopes of shedding light on one of the oldest ideals in democracy.

The emotional thread that winds through contemporary conversations about civility is in fact an ancient one. Aristotle wrote extensively about friendship in democracy and its vital importance in the underpinnings of the state. The other thread I noted—how civility is determined by and shaped through communication media—has a long history as well, although not quite as old. One might argue that the ancients, Aristotle included, thought of civility as a communication-oriented concept, evidenced by Greek and Roman interest in rhetoric and public persuasion. But given the dramatic technological changes we have seen in mass communication, it is far more useful to turn to the early-twentieth-century communication theorists Harold Innis and Marshall McLuhan, who spoke directly to the notion that available technology shapes the tenor of our times. While both were technologically determinist in their sensibilities, later scholars would pave a two-way street, demonstrating that technology and the nature of public discourse are more likely mutually reinforcing.[7]

The tensions that surround civility in the twenty-first century are great. Americans seek happiness, as is our way, but we *believe* that we seek argument, passion, and democracy along with it. How the two coexist—good feeling and discourse—is a subject that is fundamental to contemporary citizenship, regardless of our route to political participation and communication.

## Defining Civility: Virtue and Manners

While some scholars and authors have been brave enough to define "civility" and have made wonderful contributions as a result, existing definitions are imperfect, owing to the complexity of the concept. Some definitions seem a bit too intimate, focused on interpersonal interactions—how we treat our friends and neighbors, or even strangers on the street. Others are too impersonal, using high-flying rhetoric of democracy, but forgetting that citizens are living, breathing people. None of the definitions seem quite right, so scholars and writers have—logically—chosen to orient their work around definitions that make sense for the level and nature of their empirical or theoretical work. I will do the same, within the milieu of a contemporary presidential election year and its aftermath. But a detour through some of the more thoughtful works on civility is most helpful.

In an essay centered squarely on the meaning of civility in the United States, Virginia Sapiro argues—nodding to the literary critic Raymond Williams—that civility lacks proper standing in the sense of a democratic "keyword":

> Even in scholarly discussion, *civility* rests on a much looser less formalized (in any sense) set of meanings than, say, *justice*, *democracy*, or *equality*, which are the subjects of concerted efforts at definition and analysis. . . . It would take an advanced degree in alchemy, not political science, to draw a tidy but reasonably comprehensive definition out of the literatures to which one must turn to learn about civility as it is understood today.[8]

Sapiro goes on to note three types of definitions of civility. The first category focuses on politics, citizenship, and community, and is related to good character and virtue. Another group of definitions is closer to manners—civility being on the other end of a behavioral continuum from barbarism. In these definitions, self-control is of utmost importance, as civility implies regulation of the body, the emotions, and speech. The third meaning of civility, the one closest to mine for the purposes of this book, is *communicative* in nature: Civility demands arguing, listening, and respect for the deliberative process.

The first category is an important one, but as Sapiro rightly notes, it tends to bleed into citizenship and citizenly virtues. Of course, citizenship matters immensely in political theory and practice, but it has fairly well-defined components, so we can set it aside neatly as we explore civility. While the fringe contours of citizenship are subject to debate in the United States, there are some shared notions of what constitutes it—staying informed about public affairs, serving on juries when called, and so forth. This is in contrast to the more nebulous civility, which lacks a shared definitional core.

The second category outlined by Sapiro is a bit more interesting for our purposes in this book, even if not relevant at all junctures. Being civilized, having good manners, controlling one's behavior, and showing restraint in expression are necessary (even if not sufficient) for the civility needed in a strong democratic polity. Thankfully, a large number of extraordinarily talented social and cultural historians have explored the evolution of manners over time, and their work is well worth a brief discussion.

Among the most prominent historians of civility, when defined as manners and self-control, was Norbert Elias, a German sociologist who published *The Civilizing Process* in 1939.[9] Elias argued that whereas extremes of human behavior—loud conviviality, excessive crying, even uncontrolled physical occurrences such as burps and flatulence—were common and accepted for many centuries, fundamental changes in self-control emerged in the eighteenth century. This shift is in evidence throughout nineteenth-century Europe, and even in the New World, well represented by the first American president. As a young man, George Washington studied a centuries-old set of French Jesuit rules on how a person should behave.[10] Among these 110 numbered "Rules of Civility and Decent Behavior in Company and Conversation" were many related to self-control, from the mundane to the comical. A sampling:

> 5th: If You Cough, Sneeze, Sigh or Yawn, do it not Loud but Privately; and Speak not in your Yawning, but put Your handkerchief or Hand before your face and turn it aside.

> 7th: Put not off your Cloths in the presence of Others, nor go out your Chamber half Dressed.

> 16th: Do not Puff up the Cheeks, Loll not out the tongue rub the Hands, or beard, thrust out the lips, or bite them or keep the Lips too open or too Close.

But beyond bodily control and personal manners, some rules spoke to behavior in conversation, to morality, and to optimism:

> 58th: Let your Conversation be without Malice or Envy, for 'tis a Sign of a Tractable and Commendable Nature: And in all Causes of Passion admit Reason to Govern.

And finally, number 110:

> Labor to keep alive in your breast that little spark of celestial fire called conscience.

The young Washington may have found these rules helpful on a personal level, in navigating an emerging American political sphere. But most interesting is how many rules are included, and the sense of *agency* they underscore. In much the same way that contemporary self-help books and speakers emphasize the power of the individual to evoke kindness and friendship, these 110 rules of civility imply one's ability to control local environments. The implication is that, through sensitivity to social cues and self-respect, one might be virtuous, well-mannered, and perhaps even popular.

The nineteenth century saw a proliferation of books and writings on etiquette. As John Kasson notes in his study of nineteenth-century America, manuals on etiquette focused not only on practical rules, but also the control of emotions: "To conceal feelings meant to discipline them, and etiquette manuals praised such discipline as fundamental to politeness. . . . Through will and practice an individual could learn to contain eruptions of feeling just as one learned to stifle a yawn."[11]

Etiquette manuals became important as an American people tried to define itself and its class markers. Meanwhile, the most talented minds of the day turned their attention to manners and emotional control as well. Charles Darwin had a great interest in the display of emotions, as did the psychologist William James. James had developed a rather complex view of self-control, concluding that the "self" is multifaceted and that people are stage actors of sorts. Kasson argues that James's ideas foreshadow those of the twentieth-century sociologist Erving Goffman, in weaving together the psychological and the physical with the social world: "In pointing to the 'discordant splittings' of the self and the fear of discovery, James suggested the deep anxieties of daily life in a complex, segmented society. Ironically, such anxieties easily led to further role-playing as a defense—as the profusion of etiquette books eloquently testifies."[12]

Darwin and James were not the only nineteenth-century intellectuals to study politeness, although interest in sociability took wildly different forms. John Stuart Mill addressed the issue within the context of his discussion "Of Individuality" in *On Liberty*. He noted an increasingly worrisome cultural desire for what he called "moderation." In achieving a moderation of thought and behavior, a "despotism of Custom" crushes the individual: "That standard [of moderation], express or tacit, is to desire nothing strongly. Its ideal of character is to be without any marked character; to maim by compression, like a Chinese lady's foot, every part of human nature which stands out prominently."[13] Here we see a conflation of manners, custom, and public opinion, connections that Mill sped through on his way to other arguments. Would Mill have welcomed the distinct lack of manners and uncontrolled Internet discourse we now have? Perhaps. Unhealthful moderation of expression is easily overcome when we pound computer keys, alone at our screen, and beyond the confines of in-person, face-to-face interaction.

Mill's arguments about civility are rooted in his notions about conformity, and he posits that the superior person maintains individuality in the face of enormous social pressure to conform. Fearless expression of opinion defines the person of character, and constructing a society where this is possible should be the goal of all who value liberty. Mill is tackling a large number of interrelated concepts in *On Liberty*, but for our purposes he should be seen as one of the theorists least interested in manners, since manners—to his mind—buttress conformity and suppress bold ideas. As the political theorist Richard Sinopoli notes, "Mill urges upon us a thick-skinned liberalism. . . . [His] notion of civility might lead to a less 'polite' society than he lived in and for us, a society that is impolite in different ways."[14]

Conformity constrains bold opinions for most, in Mill's eyes, but it is even worse than that. Those with majority opinions are allowed to be more rude than those in the minority: "With regard to what is commonly meant by intemperate discussion, namely invective, sarcasm, personality and the like, the denunciation of these weapons would deserve more sympathy if it were ever proposed to interdict them equally to both sides; but it is only desired to restrain the employment of them against the prevailing opinion."[15]

During the same period, Alexis de Tocqueville, incisive visitor to nineteenth-century America, reflected on manners as he experienced them on his great journeys. He argued that manners in a democracy vary and stand in great contrast to the codes one finds in a European aristocracy. The sheer diversity of the American population—by class, race, region, and party—led to a situation where, in Tocqueville's words, "There is still some memory of the strict code of politeness, but no one knows quite what it said or where to find it."[16] He saw American manners as a work in progress, although he speculated that a code might be inherently impossible in a democracy:

Men [in America] have lost the common standard of manners but have not yet resolved to do without it, so each individual tries to shape, out of the ruins of former customs, some rule, however arbitrary and variable. Hence manners have neither the regularity and dignity frequent in aristocracies nor the qualities of simplicity and freedom which one sometimes finds in democracies; they are both constrained and casual.[17]

Where Tocqueville lands, in his discussion of manners, is perhaps one of the more optimistic views among all writers, of any century:

Democratic manners are neither so well thought out nor so regular [as those in aristocracies], but they often are more sincere. They form, as it were, a thin, transparent veil through which the real feelings and personal thoughts of each man can be easily seen. Hence there is frequently an intimate connection between the form and the substance of behavior; we see a less decorative picture, but one truer to life.[18]

Tocqueville wrote during a period when Americans found an abundance of manuals and essays on etiquette to guide them. On the one hand, then, there was a growing interest in polite behavior on the part of an expanding, self-conscious "respectable" class. On the other, the still-new democracy boasted the value of equality, often a difficult fit with manners, a chronic indicator of class stratification and status. Tocqueville saw that there is indeed a challenge in the flattening of manners required for a truly democratic, cross-class discourse and sensibility. He wondered if democratic conversation, an interpersonal phenomenon in his nineteenth-century world, was possible without eliminating traditional behavioral codes.

This seems a quaint matter in an age of electronic media; many of our interactions are mediated, and the "real feelings and personal thoughts of each man" are not, contra Tocqueville, so easy to sense over the Internet or airwaves. Of course, we argue with our friends, our relatives, and our coworkers. But with regard to the content of media, we cannot achieve the level of sincerity in discourse Tocqueville described.

One last nineteenth-century voice worth noting is Ferdinand Tönnies, the highly influential German social theorist, best known for his 1887 masterwork, *Gemeinschaft und Gesellschaft* (*Community and Society*). Tönnies famously argued that, over time, civilization moves from social interactions rooted in kinship and friendship to those based in commerce and contracts. With the onset of industrialization, there is a shift from ties of blood, communality, custom, and love, to markets, impersonality, self-interest, individuality, and rationality. As with Max Weber's theory of rationalization, "society" is not a particularly attractive place to Tönnies. There is a coldness about it, and we are most likely to treat others as a means to self-interested ends, rather than as persons with inherent value.[19] Tönnies pondered civility in modern society, noting that it was certainly necessary in order for markets to operate and contracts to be negotiated. The utility of civility was clear to him, but the trade-offs were also clear: Contemporary society would crush the emotional, humane remains of *gemeinschaft* (community-based) society. He notes, depressingly:

All *conventional sociability* may be understood as analogous to the exchange of material goods. The primary rule is politeness, an exchange of words and courtesies where everyone appears to be concerned for everyone else and to be esteeming each other as equals. In fact everyone is thinking of himself and trying to push his own importance and advantages at the expense of the rest.[20]

Tönnies, Weber, and their European colleagues took a dim view of civility in industrial societies, holding far more negative views than Tocqueville, who is downright sunny in comparison. Even within the varying views of civility and its motivations, nineteenth-century thinkers struggled with the nature of evolving social interactions in the context of a changing world. By doing so, they continually visit themes of this book—emotional comfort and communication as defining aspects of civility.

## Civility and Communication

My working definition for this book falls into the third category of meanings of civility delineated by Sapiro: civility as constructive engagement with others through argument, deliberation, and discourse. It is a comfortable category for many scholars, because it pulls together so much important theoretical work on political conversation (e.g., Jürgen Habermas's notion of the "public sphere"), as well as empirical work aimed at strengthening deliberation in communities (e.g., James Fishkin's "deliberative polling" or the American Association of State Colleges and Universities' American Democracy Project).[21]

Much theorizing about deliberation, as well as projects devoted to strengthening community discussion about vital issues (e.g., projects by the Kettering and Ford foundations), is interpersonal in nature: How do we talk with each other in small groups and in larger assemblies of citizens? This focus on face-to-face human interaction is important, but again, discussion is more difficult to scrutinize in online interactions. I do not mean that the literature and experiments in face-to-face political talk are irrelevant to the online democracy we now have. But we must keep in mind that what is considered "civil" in the blogosphere often would not be appropriate behavior at a city council meeting.[22]

Listening is as vital to civility as respectful talk. Although he takes on the much broader issues of American citizenship, moving far from civility, theorist Benjamin Barber reminds us that the scholarly discussion of deliberation is greatly biased toward speech. He argues that *listening* is underplayed in discussions of citizenship, and this theme will reappear repeatedly in later chapters as we focus on real cases of civility and incivility. He notes, "One measure of healthy political talk is the amount of *silence* it permits and encourages, for silence is the precious medium in which reflection is nurtured and empathy can grow. Without it, there is only the babble of raucous interests and insistent rights trying for the deaf ears of impatient adversaries."[23] How one "listens" on the Internet and where to locate silence were not questions for Barber two decades ago. Listening involves taking some time and sitting back, contemplative postures that do not fit well in our world of immediacy, impatient typing, and general communicative hyperactivity.

To say that deliberation and constructive conversation are—or should be—the defining characteristics of civility in the twenty-first century is simple enough. But we need to elaborate the concept more fully, to highlight its richness and its value. Talk is not equivalent to civility: Civility needs to be deeply and profoundly reciprocal.

More than three decades ago, long before German theorist Jürgen Habermas's work was translated and garnered American scholarly interest, before organizations like the Kettering Foundation built programs on community engagement, and when "media" meant newspapers and television, political scientist Heinz Eulau turned his considerable talents to the meaning of civility. He argued that while civility would be as elusive to define as human political behavior itself, reciprocity and mutual dependence were central components of the concept:

> The politics of civility as I think of it, refers to a broad range of potential behavioral patterns that can be expressed by such participles as persuading, soliciting, consulting, advising, bargaining, compromising, coalition-building, and so on— in other words, forms of behavior in which at least two actors

stand in a mutually dependent relationship to each other. . . . In a civil relationship, then, the interaction is reciprocal, though not necessarily symmetrical, in that both actors gain from it.[24]

This meaning of civility makes argument and deliberation central but also underscores the complexity of talk. So many of our current projects in deliberation focus on consensus-building, and that is an extraordinarily worthy goal in a nation divided by race, class, region, ethnicity, and ideology. But civility does not always succeed in producing constructive results or even closure. Civility is a process populated by agents with varying goals. Civil discourse ties agents together, whether for a moment, an election, or a lifetime. Eulau emphasized that one of the most difficult aspects of civility and civil behavior is the ability to tolerate ambiguity. Political talk, indeed our very coexistence in a democracy, demands an understanding, or tacit agreement, that clarity and consensus may not come at all.

My argument throughout this book is that we need a definition that is discursive—broad enough to include deliberation, argument, conversation, and reciprocity. But I posit that some form of emotional self-control, as well as a sense of good feeling, is just as vital to civility in our day. We need emotional restraint but also comfort if we are to engage well through communication. That is easier said than done, as we shall see in our cases that follow. How we got to this juncture, with emotional satisfaction becoming so central to civility, is a subject better left to cultural sociologists. But it seems clear that in our therapeutic society, where self-disclosure of our innermost anxieties dominates the airwaves and the bookstores, civility has great emotional content. We have to argue out differences for the sake of democracy, but we typically have to feel happy somehow while we are doing so if we are to like it or try it again. Thanks to Oprah and Dr. Phil, Americans have a far more sophisticated understanding of the complexities of daily happiness than ever before, but we have also come to seek contentment in almost all spheres.

The literature on etiquette emphasizes that manners are a chore; one needs to commit to memory—as the young George Washington did—a code of sorts. Tocqueville argued that the code is loose in a democracy; there is room for many styles and types of behavior. And these days, both make sense: We self-regulate to avoid offending people, but we cling to our rights as individuals with our own opinions, styles of expression, and so forth. These balances are central to civility, but they seem a jumble. Again, Eulau gets to the bottom of it, proposing that civility is about emotional *maturity*: "We have achieved the politics of civility when we are capable of asking not only 'What is in it for me?' but also 'What can I do for you?' It is out of these two simple questions that the maturity of civility is born."[25]

So, put another way, the emotional aspects of civility require tolerance and other-directedness. Selflessness is certainly not required, but an acknowledgement of mutuality will—in most cases—result in the good feeling we seem to need, as we argue about politics in our time.

## A Note on Deliberation

Some of the most interesting work in political theory over the last decade has revolved around democratic deliberation—how we come to make decisions, whether in legislative, judicial, or community settings. Of course, the study of conversation and talk has a long pedigree, with serious attention in the late nineteenth century from Tocqueville and Gabriel Tarde, the French social theorist. Civility and deliberation are not nearly the same concepts, since deliberation is typically an activity aimed at resolution of disputes or conflicts. We deliberate in advance of a decision to be made, typically, and those who study this sort of talk do so with an interest in the ultimate quality of our decisions.

Despite this focus on decisions, some key aspects of deliberation are of interest in the study of civility. In particular, Amy Gutmann and Dennis Thompson's notion of "civic magnanimity" highlights aspects of civility that explore new territory.[26] First, civic magnanimity demands an acknowledgment of the moral status of someone else's position. It also calls for a degree of open-mindedness, during the deliberative process. Finally, they argue, to achieve magnanimity, citizens should seek an "economy of moral disagreement" whereby they try to minimize conflict where possible and seek consensus, while not necessarily compromising one's position.

This is important and heady stuff, outlining the ideals a good society might strive toward. It is too grand a standard for the more base, simple civility I discuss in this book. But it is important to be cognizant of the higher-level principles for political behavior that have characterized normative views of citizen deliberation. Perhaps these principles have more value in the practice of civility than is typically evident during campaigns and other moments where talk is talk and there is no immediate, prescribed aim or decision point. It is an issue we take up later, especially with regard to the nebulous journalistic standards we find in contemporary media coverage of political candidates.

## So Which Is It? Are We More Civil or Less Civil?

Without question, the dominant strain in the literatures on both manners and political civility has been a struggle over the *trend*: Is civility on the decline? Journalists, scholars, and statesman have asked the question repeatedly in different venues and for varying purposes. This discussion takes on many forms. During presidential campaigns, for example, we ask whether the nasty mudslinging is a new phenomenon. Inevitably, a historian points out that things were worse in the eighteenth or nineteenth century, and that assertion is either believed or not.

Most scholars and writers—apart from cultural historians like Elias and Kasson, who have seen manners as contextually bound—have bemoaned a decline of civility in American politics and social life. This ruefulness is a shame, since so many historians have documented phenomena to disprove this view, such as the horrendous dirty presidential campaigning of the past. (Thomas Jefferson and John Adams attacked each other viciously; Lyndon Johnson's "Daisy" ads against Barry Goldwater were quite over the top.) But I suppose the popular logic goes something like this, even if it does not match history: We have gone "downhill," but we can regain that civility, an American ideal we somehow lost over time.

In any case, the alleged decline of civility, of manners, and the public sphere in the United States more generally, has captured the imagination of the academy and Americans well beyond college campuses. One writer who has made the strong argument for a decline is Stephen Carter, law professor and novelist. Carter believes that the American civility decline began dramatically in the 1960s.[27] He argues that, before the 1960s, there was a "golden age" in the United States where people generally held the same dreams for the American experience. It is not so much that life before the 1960s was better, he posits. But there was a shared creed about America, and it was diminished by the Vietnam War and the student movement. John Kennedy, Martin Luther King, and Robert Kennedy were assassinated, and division—not solidarity—prevailed. Carter bemoans the destruction of a common morality and set of values, and notes

> As the sixties swept into the seventies, leaving behind the wreckage of the illusion, there was nothing available to put in its place: no shared meanings, no shared commitments, none of the social glue that makes a people a people. . . . Having abandoned the illusion of commonality, we have adopted an even more dangerous illusion: that social norms are not important and thus we can do as we like.[28]

The most compelling empirically based arguments about our decline have come from the sociologist Robert Putnam. While his "bowling alone" hypothesis spurred a rancorous debate and significant criticism from many quarters, the contributions he has made to current discourse are extraordinarily valuable and worth our time here. Putnam is concerned broadly with social life in America, but his arguments about how we treat each other in daily life are certainly relevant to a study on political civility.[29]

While Putnam takes on a variety of topics in the general arena of social life and culture, he is interested in civility as it is manifest in altruistic behavior. Hence he studies volunteerism, philanthropy, and other forms of individual contributions to neighborhood and community. He also studies polite behavior toward faceless "others." One of the premier examples from his enormously popular *Bowling Alone* is the decline in number of drivers who obey stop signs, an intriguing indicator of how people act, not toward others directly, but toward fellow citizens *in theory*. He notes that, according to studies of New York intersections with stop signs: "In 1979, 37 percent of all motorists made a full stop, 34 percent a rolling stop, and 29 percent no stop at all. By 1996, 97 percent made no stop at all at the very same intersections."[30]

Attacks on Putnam—his propositions and data—are abundant and vehement in many scholarly circles. But so is the chronic appeal of his decline argument, hence the attention he has received. I do not hope to settle long-running debates over the "bowling alone" thesis here, but it seems clear from the historical literature pioneered by Elias that arguments about decline are a bit dangerous when it comes to political civility. We have many well-documented cases of incivility, from well over two centuries of American electoral politics (poor Martin Van Buren, already vice president, was accused of wearing a woman's corset!), not to mention outstanding cases of incivility by sitting statesmen, such as Senator Joseph McCarthy's performances and the hearings of the House Un-American Activities Committee in the 1950s.

These moments in American history underscore to us just how disrespectful, worrisome, and downright mean political discourse has been in our past. To argue that we do much better today is a difficult proposition to uphold. But it is not clear that we do worse either.

What is easier to argue is that the uncivil tendencies in American culture are more apparent and abundant thanks to pervasive media. One might have been able to ignore gruesome partisan bickering in the early nineteenth century simply by neglecting the newspaper or avoiding the local tavern. But the "in your face" quality of contemporary media makes this avoidance impossible: We wait in airport gates, car washes, and doctors' offices with the blare of CNN keeping us company, even if we would prefer a different soundtrack as we go about our business.

So I will not argue here that civility has declined—clearly the most popular argument these days—or is on the rise. Neither assertion seems supportable, and both are far too broad to be stated definitively. What we can do, however, is document the tendencies and tools related to civility and incivility, and try to make sense of what they mean for American political culture.

## Plan for the Book

The chapters to come elaborate the three arguments made in this chapter: that civility and incivility are best seen as strategic assets, that comfort (or discomfort) is a critical component of civility, and that we somehow must reconcile both these notions with the demand for communicative interactivity brought to us by the Internet.

Chapter 2 is devoted to one fascinating aspect of the 2008 presidential campaign—the candidacy of Alaska's governor, Sarah Palin, for the vice presidency. Interest in this new player on the national political scene was intense, and she received attention and scrutiny— good and bad—at a level we rarely see for either a vice presidential or even a presidential candidate. Some of this attention was rooted in novelty, as a new political face is always intriguing. But this novelty was exacerbated by her being the first female Republican vice presidential candidate, her attractiveness, and her ability to give a rousing speech, as well as the generally exciting nature of the campaign itself. To say that she received great attention is a tremendous understatement: She was discussed across millions of households and work-places, and was a constant focus of media attention. In our time, the number of "hits" one receives on a search engine like Google is a fine indicator of public interest. In their annual wrap-up, the 2008 Year-End Zeitgeist, the Google management noted that Governor Palin took first place honors as the most "googled" person in the world, fol-lowed by "Beijing 2008" (the Olympics) and the Facebook log-in site. President Obama held down the number-six slot, while neither his running mate nor his opponent even appears on the top-ten list.[31]

There are, as a result of Palin's visibility in the campaign, multi-ple points of scholarly interest—gender dynamics, the place of Alaska in a national political context, and the role of leadership background among executive-level candidates in the United States. In Chapter 2, however, my focus is solely on speeches that Palin delivered, the nature of her campaign rallies across the country, and the media reac-tion to her rallies. Her well-attended campaign events are a useful arena for studying civility, rich in dynamics: the composition and behavior of the crowds, her rhetorical style, the interaction between her and her audiences, and how journalists portrayed these events. My empirical analysis shows that the media did tend to focus on the least civil of her behaviors, for better or worse. But it also shows that Palin's rhetorical approach opened up opportunities for citizen expression that were unusual and difficult for journalists to parse. Based on scrutiny of news articles about Palin's events, I argue that journalists spent an inappropriately large amount of time and energy on incivility at Palin rallies, given the paucity of truly uncivil behav-ior they encompassed.

Chapter 3 analyzes our new president's words, as he took the stage for a highly charged address on civility—his 2009 commence-ment address at the University of Notre Dame. The president was invited by the university president to speak in South Bend, and the invitation set off a firestorm of controversy. Vocal alumni and stu-dents, as well as Catholics far beyond campus, were appalled that a president who had been an outspoken advocate of abortion rights and stem cell research would both address graduates and accept an honorary degree. Although many presidents had been invited to do the same in Notre Dame's storied past, none had the documented record of conflict with Catholic doctrine that Obama had, from his published work to his campaign speeches. America and the world watched the speech with great anticipation that May afternoon, and the president took the opportunity to speak directly about abortion and civility. His success in moving us toward that elusive "common ground" remains to be seen over the coming years. But I argue that the speech reveals much about his perspective on American civility, as well as the nature of public opinion in the United States. The Notre Dame address is full of promise and ideas, ideas that may very well shape the Obama presidency itself.

Only a few months after Obama spoke about civility at Notre Dame, he was confronted with a far more complex set of issues surrounding civility, with the appearance of often violent health care "town hall meetings" in the summer of 2009. While it is unclear just how many raucous meetings occurred, the scenes of yelling and screaming, between members of Congress and constituents, dominated the news and the Web. Obama was forced to recognize the nature of these town meetings and what they might mean for civility. So in Chapter 3, I also review the health care debates during 2009, an arena where both Obama and Palin found themselves playing a starring role.

The final empirical chapter is about our American future—the young people raised on the Internet. Any study of civility should pay substantial attention to young people, given the vital nature of political socialization in a civil society.[32] Adults, be they citizens, journalists, or politicians, have their own ideas about civility, but without an intense focus on our newest generation of citizens, we have few clues about the future. I attempt to map their struggles with civility, anxieties that will be broader American struggles as these young people mature. I aggregated opinions of college students from more than thirty college and university campuses across the state of Georgia—from small, rural two-year institutions to large urban research universities (Georgia State University and Georgia Institute of Technology) to a land-grant institution, the University of Georgia. Colleagues and I collected these data in the spring of 2008 and again in 2009, in response to state legislative concerns about free speech, in particular to fears that some students were not able to express their opinions in the classroom and in public spaces.

While I found nothing particularly worrisome related to free speech, or at least no patterns that ran counter to what one typically finds in higher education, I did find—in response to open-ended queries—tremendous unhappiness with civility. Students complained about each other most of all, and this was an intriguing result for a study originally focused on faculty-student interaction. The diversity of students in the study, opining during a very contentious election year and the subsequent spring, is a magnificent setting in which to explore civil behavior and conversation. One wonders, with these study results, how we can build a culture of polite argument, given the negative way students view each other when political tensions run high.

In closing, I raise the earlier question one last time: Is there a danger in my approach—treating civility and incivility as tactics or strategies? Can this perspective demean American politics, making civility seem less valuable and important? I do not believe so. As I will argue in the concluding chapter, seeing civility as a tool can enable citizens and leaders to approach their activities with more self-consciousness and more care. When we think about what we do and realize our own agency, there is an opportunity for greater integrity of action and attention to real democratic ideals.

While civility in politics is a concept with many faces and my case studies probe only a few aspects of it, they are helpful in understanding the challenges we face as Americans. Are we prone to incivility in our discourse? What does it actually look like, and how much does it matter? How do different actors on the political stage approach civility, be they journalists, our elected officials, or the college students who will one day set the tone for American citizenship and leadership? This book hopes to shed light on areas we must explore, given the imperatives of democratic theory and the need to enhance political life as best we can.

I shall not close with a definitive meaning of civility, since its meaning will always be tied to the changing nature of social relations. What was civil and acceptable in the nineteenth century is often uncivil today, and the same may well be true in the future. Taking on a grand concept like civility may seem outrageously ambitious, but in the end I hope to develop and value it in a way that fits our immensely complicated moment in political culture.

# 2 / Sarah Palin and Her Publics

[This] political absurdity, the "politics of personal
destruction" . . . [i]t's pretty insane—my staff and I
spend most of our day dealing with this instead of
progressing our state now. I know I promised no more
"politics as usual," but this isn't what anyone had in
mind for Alaska.

> GOVERNOR SARAH PALIN,
> announcing her resignation, July 3, 2009

To Alaskans—both allies and adversaries—Sarah
Palin, 44, is known as "Sarah Barracuda," a nickname
that goes back to her days as an aggressive basketball
player.

> KEITH EPSTEIN, "McCain's VP Choice:
> 'Sarah Barracuda,'" *Business Week*

Interesting new candidates on the political scene often open up old
issues in novel ways, and that was certainly the case with former
Governor Sarah Palin's 2008 vice presidential run. As a younger
politician, still in her mid-40s, and the first Republican woman on
a presidential ticket, she garnered special attention from the public and the media. In the midst of an already complex and exciting
race, Palin's candidacy added yet another element to the debate. Her
strong persona also intensified journalistic scrutiny in unusual ways
that give us much to ponder. Putting aside media interest, Palin's cha-
risma, her approach to political speech, and her ambivalence about
the role of gender, all provide a tremendously rich portrait of civility
and incivility in public life.

In this chapter, after a brief tour through some relevant literature about collective behavior and public opinion, I evaluate Palin's vice presidential speech making and the media coverage of her behavior in large public venues. While there are a variety of angles from which to view a complex figure—indeed phenomenon—like Palin, among the most striking was her ability to make strong emotional connections with audiences, both in person and through televised performances. So my focus here is primarily on those connections, with close reading of journalistic commentary and Internet chatter. The observation that Palin represents extraordinarily effective uses of both civility and incivility as strategic assets is key to the themes of this book. But I also look closely at the responses she elicits and the appeals to emotion in her words and tone, two other vital components of how civility is conceptualized in our times. Palin has a knack for reciprocity and interchange, which are critical in developing norms of civility. Her style is highly conflict oriented, but at the same time provides the communicative comfort that binds supporters to her with great intensity.

Sarah Palin is, I argue, a breakthrough candidate in being able to carry out rhetorical "multitasking" that is unique. She has been rabid, mean-spirited, catty, empathic, warm, humane, and engaging, all at the same time. Many orators—male and female—have had these same talents. But in our time, she is unique for her historical candidacy and her particularized appeal. Her impact on American politics may be fleeting or last for decades, but Sarah Palin—in the fall of 2008—was one of the shrewdest strategic users of both civility and incivility. And it is her success in these dimensions, so unusual for a woman leader, that both awed journalists and made them uniquely punishing.

## Civility, Social Glue, and Crowds

In Chapter 1, I traced some of the varying perspectives on civility over time with a focus on manners but also on political discourse. Another aspect of civility, best described by sociologists, is its binding power. Scholars have long argued that civility does not simply make for better politics, policy, congressional sessions, town meetings, or workplace "watercooler" discussions about politics. And civility is certainly not primarily about etiquette, although manners do matter, at least in American culture as it has evolved. How civil or uncivil a society actually is can be correlated, sociologists argue, with nothing less than the stability and progress of a nation.

Social order—the constellation of institutions, norms, and practices in any given society—is what enables communities to achieve persistence through time. How long a regime or culture exists is determined in great part by tacit agreement about "the way things work," and when dissension (or even revolution) starts to question the existing order, fundamental change in institutions and practices is not far behind. As Dennis Peck explains, the link between civility and social order is an ancient one:

> Civility is central to any discussion of order. The terms *citizenship*, *civility*, and *civilization* are derived from the Latin *civis* (citizen) and *civitas* (city) and are the equivalents of the Greek words stemming from *polis* (city). From the classical perspective, the civilized are those who are fit to live in cities, fit to experience both the benefits and responsibilities of citizenship, and are political.[1]

Civility is what enables the social order to exist, and therefore makes possible the very functioning of a city, state, or nation. This point seems clear, but it is the binding of people to each other that sociologists are most interested in; hence they emphasize the importance of authority (it organizes and maintains groups), the recognition of a collective good, and self-control. Most helpful to us is the emphasis on interactivity and "connectedness": Social order and the civility it demands function through networks, groups, neighborhoods, Internet blogs, Facebook, and other means. Connection is an important theme in contemporary civility, whether the bonds are established in person or over the Web.

It is not a leap to argue, as many have, that social glue is a way to think about public opinion. In our time, we may think that opinion poll data or the content of leading Internet blogs is synonymous with public opinion and that public opinion is typically divided. But in previous eras, public opinion was often seen as an implicit social consensus or set of well-understood behavioral norms. The notion that public opinion can be seen as social glue was popularized in the late twentieth century by the German researcher Elisabeth Noelle-Neumann, but it was introduced earliest and with most force by John Locke in his 1690 *Essay Concerning Human Understanding*. It is here that Locke argues for a "law of opinion"—what psychologists now call social norms—and its tremendous power to bind people together in a common culture. Locke wrote that people cannot exist in social isolation because of the pain it entails:

> Solitude many men have sought, and been reconciled to: but nobody that has the least thought or sense of a man about him, can live in society under the constant dislike and ill opinion of his familiars, and those he converses with. This is a burden too heavy for human sufferance: and he must be made up of irreconcilable contradictions, who can take pleasure in company, and yet be insensible of contempt and disgrace from his companions.[2]

Rousseau would offer his notion of a "general will" in the eighteenth century—a somewhat more complex interpretation of social consensus—and others would follow. These meanings of public opinion are out of fashion in twenty-first-century American political culture, as we tend to see ourselves as unified as a nation, but also deeply divided by party, race, class, generation, and other demographic and cultural partitions.

Within our divisions and subdivisions, however, social glue and bonding of people is as important as it was during Locke's and earlier eras. Our groups and social enclaves, neighborhoods or faceless citizens posting on the Internet, still rely on the desire and ability of people to form organizations. One organization of a sort, common during presidential campaigns, more sporadic during other periods, is the political rally, march, or gathering. We can trace the notion of public demonstration back to the seventeenth century, but political gatherings organized by parties and campaign organizations are creatures that appeared with regularity and great vigor in nineteenth-century America.[3] Today, they are enhanced and brought to an international audience by television coverage and YouTube. Rallies and demonstrations are, as sociologist Robert Merton called them, "temporary aggregations" of public opinion—crowds coming together for the express purpose of political speech and participation. While candidate Barack Obama drew tremendously large and excitable crowds during 2008, it is fair to say that Palin's were far more interesting to the public opinion analyst.

## Crowds, Politics, and Palin

Sarah Palin may be a gifted orator with an admirable ability to move audiences. But crowds at political gatherings during election years have been interesting to students of American politics for the content of speeches (e.g., the Lincoln-Douglas debates), for figuring out how to report crowd sizes, and for the behavior of individuals in attendance. As we have seen, mass rallies, parades, and political festivals were abundant in nineteenth-century America, enlivening the popular politics of the age, particularly at century's end.[4]

Contemporary political rallies have some commonalities with gatherings of previous centuries—there is often a carnival-type atmosphere, intense partisanship, booing, hissing, and sustained applause. The differences are greater, however. Today's political rally is often captured on video by professional journalistic organizations or amateurs, people do not take arduous, muddy trips on horseback to rally sites, and in great contrast to the nineteenth century, giant video screens enable those distant from the stage to hear and see the speaker, and thus participate more fully in the event.

Although political gatherings and rallies held an important place in eighteenth- and nineteenth-century American politics, these were not of particular interest as a class of phenomena until the turn of the twentieth century. In the late nineteenth century, the budding field of sociology began to study collective behavior, led in many ways by Gustave Le Bon, who published *The Crowd* in 1895. *The Crowd* has been an extraordinarily influential work, even if somewhat under-theorized and lacking in empirical detail. As Robert Merton argued in his introduction to the 1960 edition, it may be best to think of the book, with its many wonderful observations, as describing the behavior of crowds and mobs more than explaining them. In fact, Sigmund Freud was highly critical of the book for just this reason and had his own notions of crowd psychology, entailing repression, hero worship, and other psychological dynamics. Freud was not the only thinker to take issue with Le Bon and his methods, but *The Crowd*—for all its deficits—has been one of the most influential books in social psychology.[5]

Le Bon argues that a crowd—either gathered for a preordained purpose or gathering spontaneously—can at times become much like a single being, erasing individuals. A crowd can be a "group mind" of sorts:

> Whoever be the individuals that compose it, however like or unlike be their mode of life, their occupations, their character or their intelligence, the fact that they have been transformed into a crowd puts them in possession of a sort of collective mind which makes them feel, think, and act in a manner quite different from that in which each individual of them would feel, think, and act were he in a state of isolation.[6]

In crowds, individuals can become suggestible, emotional, less cautious, and even barbaric, as a result of the anonymity they feel around them. Le Bon is most famous for the related notion of "contagion": Emotions are passed quickly from one crowd member to another, as with a virus, and this contagion is compelling and not easily resisted. He even calls this feeling of being caught up in the collective mind of a crowd "hypnotic," leading people to act in ways that are entirely out of character. While he seemed taken with the most extreme of crowd behaviors (such as violence), Le Bon's insights are still useful in thinking about political rallies. His general point, that people feel differently—often freer and more intensely emotional—when enveloped in an excited crowd, is a vital one. Later research and theory in psychology—the diffusion of responsibility, convergence theory, emerging norms theory, and other theses related to conformity—would support many of Le Bon's conclusions. In fact, there is little question that crowds can carry one away, alter one's behavior, and create a sort of intensity hard to generate in a small group of individuals.[7]

In much the same vein that Emile Durkheim, a contemporary of Le Bon, noted the totemic power of the flag to inspire bravery and emotion, Le Bon focused on rhetoric and symbols. He argued, as others have, that vague words are often the most compelling and can be extraordinarily useful to those trying to persuade a crowd:

> Words whose sense is the most ill-defined are sometimes those that posses the most influence. Such, for example, are the terms democracy, socialism, equality, liberty, etc. . . . They synthesise the most diverse unconscious aspirations and the hope of their realization. Reason and arguments are incapable of combating certain words and formulas.[8]

Le Bon's work was intriguing at the time he published it, but later events would make it even more engaging: The twentieth century would witness all manner of mobs and crowds, from Nazi-inspired rallies in the 1930s to the crowds of American social movements three decades later. As crowds, demonstrators, and mobs became increasingly complex and diverse, social theory and research became far more sophisticated. Le Bon opened up an area that would be, for a while at least, among the most productive in social psychology. These literatures are too vast to review here, but suffice it to say we now have an impressive—albeit still incomplete—understanding of how factors like anonymity in a crowd and persuasive appeals by an orator can lead to unexpected behaviors, from the humanitarian to the horrific.[9]

For our purposes in trying to understand Sarah Palin and the reaction to her, Le Bon, Gabriel Tarde, Elias Canetti, and others who probed the worrisome power of crowds are wonderfully instructive.[10] Le Bon in particular captures the emotional volatility of crowds— that feeling one can get at a concert, rally or demonstration—that we changed somehow, stepped outside our normal self. That a crowd can develop a "group mind" sounds like an absurdity, of course, particularly in this age of neuroscience and the plethora of evidence about unique, individual cognitive development. Yet there is no question that most people are capable of being swept away, unmoored from their usual patterns of thought or action, and can join a wave with real joy. These somewhat mysterious but powerful dynamics, what Le Bon thought of as "contagion," were major drivers in Palin's appeal and impact. Journalists recognized the dynamic as unusual, at least for a U.S. presidential election campaign, as did Palin's supporters and detractors.

In fact, I would argue that Palin reinvented the very notion of the crowd for our time, capitalizing on her talents to encourage a new degree of public behavioral intensity. Her rallies produced a strong air of unpredictability that ratcheted up both the intensity and the subsequent media scrutiny. Journalists conveyed a sense that "anything could happen" at a Palin rally, and this is, of course, the best sort of news to increase viewers' interest. Then-Senator Barack Obama's campaign rallies of 2008—during the primaries and the general election campaign—incorporated many of the same elements as the Palin rallies: intense partisan emotion and immense size. But Palin's crowds were characterized by the media as frightening, whether they were in fact dangerous or not. And with perceived danger comes journalistic excitement and carelessness in reporting, as we will see in the next section.

## Palin Rallies and the Media

Palin's rallies were outstanding with regard to size and character, as she campaigned hard during the fall of 2008. Her rise to celebrity status began in late August when Senator John McCain, whose somewhat flailing summer presidential campaign reenergized itself by announcing Palin as his running mate just before the Republican convention. In introducing America to the Alaska governor, McCain emphasized her success as a reformer, and Palin made reform a key part of her convention speech days later. Her September 3 convention speech emphasized her outsider status, along with references to her background, her family, and her admiration for Senator McCain:

> I pledge to all Americans that I will carry myself in this spirit as vice president of the United States. This was the spirit that brought me to the governor's office, when I took on the old politics as usual in Juneau . . . when I stood up to the special interests, the lobbyists, big oil companies, and the good-ol' boys network.
>
> Sudden and relentless reform never sits well with entrenched interests and power brokers. That's why true reform is so hard to achieve.[11]

Viewed by over 37 million people, the speech was widely seen by partisans in both major parties as a tremendous success. A *U.S. News and World Report* article collected a range of print and broadcast media reactions to the speech, these samples among them:

> On CBS, Jeff Greenfield said she "made a very strong first impression, the kind Republicans want appealing to people beyond the base." On NBC, Brian Williams referred to

a "tough and warmly received speech," while on MSNBC, David Gregory said, "I think this was a very strong presentation. . . . If this was a first test for . . . Palin on the national stage . . . then she's gone a long way toward being very successful." On CNN, Wolf Blitzer said, "She really did hit it out of the park tonight not only here but for millions of Americans watching across the country. No doubt . . . their first real impression of her had to be very, very positive given this speech that was obviously very carefully written but very well delivered." Anderson Cooper [also of CNN] added, "If anyone is wondering why she is such a popular governor in the state of Alaska, you saw the answer tonight."[12]

The convention speech was a success on multiple dimensions: It introduced a large swath of voters to the potential vice president, rallied the convention attendees to great effect, and charmed a cynical national media, at least temporarily. But success in a convention speech, given before a friendly and highly engaged audience, is hardly impressive to scholars of political communication. A passionately positive reaction is expected and very often delivered. Yet a new face, in a highly contested election, and a female one at that, most definitely generated a spark in the early days of the general election campaign. Palin was off and running as a campaigner of great promise in an election that promised to be a close one.

In our time, with broadcast cable media, TiVo, YouTube, and many other venues for viewing speeches in real time and at one's leisure, Americans have seemingly endless opportunities to see politicians directly and on demand. No doubt the audience for full speeches and clips of speeches has skyrocketed in ways we cannot measure. But even with this direct access to an orator's political rhetoric, we still rely on our journalists, pundits, and commentators. The interpretation of the political world is booming. We have incredibly successful Internet sites like the Huffington Post, with its mix of credentialed journalists, celebrities who write about politics, and regular folks with opinions, contributing essays and posts to blogs. The Web site Technorati, which monitors the popularity of blogs, uses one measure they call "Authority" that counts the number of blogs linking to a Web site over the previous six months. The Huffington Post tops the list of 100 influential blogs—influential by this measure at least—with an Authority score of 21,949 (for comparison sake, the CNN Ticker blog is 42nd out of 100 with a score of 3,241, and *Entertainment Weekly* is at 76, with 2,037 linking blogs).[13]

I examine the content of some popular blogs later in the chapter, to get a better sense of the partisan concerns about Palin. But first I focus on conventional mainstream media—CNN and Fox News. These were the two most popular cable networks for campaign news in 2008: In October 2008, the Pew Research Center found that 25 percent of Americans surveyed turned to CNN as a main source and 21 percent viewed Fox. I also evaluated coverage in the *New York Times*, for its high daily circulation (well over two million readers) and its status as the "paper of record" in the eyes of many political elites and journalists.[14]

There is not quite a straight line from crowds to media coverage: Crowds gather in a real physical space, and that geographic location matters. Palin's crowds—those "temporary aggregations of the public," in Merton's wonderful language—were in many ways typical of the rally participants one sees in the autumn heat of a close presidential contest. They were engaged and rowdy, and part of this excitement was due to being a *chosen* geographic venue. Campaign schedules, particularly in the fall of a presidential race, are always changing, as political strategists try to figure out how best to use the precious time of exhausted candidates. Campaigns figure out where (down to the county) they need to boost a candidate's image. The places a candidate visits are hot, clearly, and this fact gives crowd behavior an added intensity. And while no one speech in any one city or town will necessarily move numbers dramatically there, there is a chance for productive publicity, as local television covers the event and word of mouth about the event spreads through neighborhoods and workplaces. There is method to what looks like the madness of candidate hopscotching around the nation to address audiences, and Palin's consultants kept her on the move to make the most of her appeal.

The cable television coverage and articles in the *Times* devoted to the Palin rallies were textured and complex, and therefore not easily coded or put in categories in the typical manner of news content analysis. This could be done, but we would lose all subtlety, context, and argument among commentators, so I chose the less sterile method of close reading to locate themes in the coverage. CNN and the *New York Times* made attempts to balance coverage of the rallies, while Fox transparently took a more partisan approach. Fox, in contrast to the other outlets, often mentioned the (perceived) unfair nature of Palin rally coverage by other outlets, and also questioned whether they were unusual crowds. A typical comment from cohost Fred Barnes of Fox's *The Beltway Boys*:

> You know, I'm appalled at the double standard that the media is applying to crowds at campaign rallies. They have created this myth that the Republican crowds are enraged and calling for blood. But they don't report the kind of stuff . . . where [Obama] protesters scream things I can't repeat now, holding up signs that say abort Sarah Palin, and much, much worse. There's a huge double standard here.[15]

And on *Fox News Sunday*, we have this exchange among commentators (Chris Wallace is the host, Brit Hume is a *Fox* editor):

> **Wallace:** So, Brit, what about this whole controversy about the anger of the crowds at McCain rallies and the rhetoric that has come from McCain and Palin? Do you think it's over the line?
>
> **Hume:** The rhetoric or the crowds?
>
> **Wallace:** Well, both, the rhetoric from the candidates and the rhetoric from the crowds.

**Hume:** Well, as [McCain campaign manager] Rick Davis was saying, they let anybody who wants to come into those rallies and town hall meetings come in. And if you do that, you get what you get. Obviously, there are some people who are alarmed by Obama, but I don't think for a moment that the issues that have been raised by the McCain campaign and the things that he has said are over the top in terms of political rhetoric, I mean, it's been intense, it's mean, it's been intense, it's been feisty, it's been at times harsh and negative, but over the line, I don't think so.

**Mara Liasson** [of *National Public Radio*, a few seconds later]: I do think, however, when you read stories that somebody at a Palin rally yelled, "Kill him," or, "Off with his head" [referring to Obama] or something like that, it is incumbent upon the candidates, either at that rally if they hear it or at least at the next public event, to say something, the way McCain did in that town meeting, to kind of make sure that they set the tone the way they want to.[16]

These are brief snippets of larger conversations on Fox News, also found in other venues (such as the Sunday morning news programs), that reflect some limited soul-searching on the part of partisan and nonpartisan journalists and pundits about the coverage of the rallies. Most of the journalists had some trouble parsing audience reaction and campaign rhetoric of candidates Palin and McCain (as in the second conversation). In fact, this was a recurring challenge of the coverage throughout the fall, aggravating a chicken-egg fashion: Who pushed whom? Was the candidate throwing out the "red meat" of political attack and the audience simply responding gleefully? Or was the candidate delivering a speech too focused, or uninterested to hear inappropriate audience reaction? Or did the candidates hear problematic audience reaction and choose to ignore it?

These questions cannot be answered through the coverage I analyzed and are likely difficult to answer even by the most objective witness to these rallies, given the loud and often chaotic forum of a campaign event. Some journalists, as we see later in this chapter, argued that there was in fact a detectable pattern of bad behavior at the Palin rallies. But it is important to point out here that journalists—particularly those with the most airtime and influence (hosts of talk shows, participants in roundtables)—had great difficulty separating speaker and audience, for motives and behavior. The same problem worried Gustave Le Bon a hundred years ago: Do audience and orator become part of a conflated "group mind," nearly indistinguishable from each other? Our analysts in these Fox transcripts experience the same problem disentangling whether to call out the audience or the candidate for critique.

Journalists and anchors seem puzzled enough that in one CNN news program anchor T. J. Holmes, looking for some assistance in disentangling candidate from audience, questions an undecided voter named Cynthia Hudson. Holmes asks Hudson what she thought of McCain's attempt, after hearing a rally audience member demean Obama, to inject "some civility, some calm, some respect into a race you've noticed has gotten nasty":

**Holmes:** What do you see out there . . . Cynthia?

**Hudson:** I appreciated what he [McCain] did say [to the audience member]. But I would have liked to have seen Governor Palin say it. [It] seems that most of her followers and her rallies is where all of this happens. So we haven't heard from her yet.

**Holmes:** Do you think that candidates are trying to, or are we talking about the Republicans here, are trying to fire the [Republican voter] base up in that way, or just they're playing politics? And you have some people out there, you can't control your voters, you can't control what everybody says or what they do.

**Hudson:** Well, I think that they actually kind of played into that. And I think that Governor Palin really pulled that out of the crowd. I don't think that they just came and said—

but the way she talks and how she—is against Obama and her rhetoric kind of pulls that out of the crowd.[17]

The Palin rallies, and what seems to be a conflation of candidate-orator and audience, confused journalists to the point where they enlisted nonjournalists to help interpret the nature of the crowds. This struggle in the news coverage was notable, making a bit more real the notion of a "group mind"—a mass of frenzied believers and leader, bound together across their roles as participant and orator by psychic electricity.

## Anger, Incivility, and Hate

The bulk of substantive Palin-related transcripts and articles I have reviewed from the fall of 2008 were focused on the negative aspects of her rallies or on the defenses of negativity that we saw at Fox. Sometimes this focus is brief; sometimes it is lengthy and intense. Of particular interest are attacks by the candidate on her opponents and the rabid reaction these attacks seemed to engender among rally attendees. CNN anchor Don Lemon noted:

Well, some of these rallies are getting rowdy, crowds of John McCain and Sarah Palin's events have taken a turn toward anger, to say the very least. People are attacking Barack Obama, shouting "terrorist" and "off with his head." The comments are off mike and hard to hear, but take a listen to the tone [video clip of McCain begins].[18]

*New York Times* reporter Julie Bosman, covering Palin in Florida, wrote from Jacksonville in early October:

Standing before a sea of red T-shirts and homemade signs reading "No Communists!" and "Palin's Pitbulls," Ms. Palin on Tuesday nestled in to her Republican base. "Our opponent voted to cut off funding for our troops," Ms. Palin said, as she was interrupted by a deep-throated chorus of boos. "He did this even after saying that he wouldn't do such a thing. And he said too, that our troops in Afghanistan are just, quote, 'air-raiding villages and killing civilians.' I hope Americans know that is not what our brave men and women are doing in Afghanistan."

"Treason!" one man in the crowd shouted angrily. . . . From Jacksonville in the northeast to Pensacola in the Panhandle, the fiery crowds gathered to jeer at any hint of liberalism, boo loudly at the mere mention of Senator Barack Obama's name and heckle the traveling press corps (at a rally in Clearwater, one man hurled a racial epithet at a television cameraman).[19]

And in this transcript, CNN's Campbell Brown introduces an October Palin rally news clip:

> **Brown:** In a moment, we're going to go deep inside the crowd that packed Sarah Palin's campaign rally in Virginia today. We're going to hear from some of Palin's loyal supporters, some of them getting very emotional, when we come back.
> [Video clip of rally, NASCAR track in Virginia Beach]
> **Voice of Hank Williams, Jr.,** Singer, McCain Supporter: John and Sarah tell you just what they think. And they're not going to blink. And they don't have terrorist friends to whom their careers are linked.
> **Brown:** Some tough stuff there. . . . Sarah Palin no longer saying Barack Obama pals around with terrorist. So you can see some of her supporters are, but she is giving her fans plenty of red meat to chew over.[20]

These are but a few samples of the Palin rally coverage in the news, and there are, of course, thousands more, some reporting offensive chants like "John McCain. Not Hussein," for example, a reference to Obama's middle name.[21]

What is interesting in the media reports about the Palin campaign is the focus on what seem to be singular moments, chants, or jeers from the audiences: I found no reports where journalists try to determine the percentage of the crowd yelling offensive slogans, or even an attempt to figure out whether problematic behavior was undertaken by organized groups, or were just spontaneous rhetorical outbursts of unconnected strangers. It is difficult, as any campaign journalist will note, to study large crowds in a systematic fashion. But in the Palin coverage we see a distinct *lack of interest* in any sort of quantitative analysis of particularly venomous elements in the crowds. This was, without question, a failing of the popular news media during the campaign, and one wonders why, besides difficulty, even occasional attempts at more precision are absent. One answer is that the news frame of Palin as flinger of "red meat," with no interest (indeed a purposeful ignoring) in disciplining the crowds she drew, engaged viewers and readers. As a result of this inability to cover crowds with precision, we have little sense of the normality of Palin's crowds. We have no idea whether her supporters were more or less worrisome, relative to Democratic crowds. This question seemed to be of no interest to CNN, for example, despite the resources the network commanded.

The comparative issue—whether Palin's crowds were angrier, meaner, and more uncivil than those of other candidates in the fall of 2008—is lost to us now, with the events "old news" at this point. But the omission of comparative analysis is glaring and lends credence to the complaints of Fox analysts, even if they too failed in comparative crowd analysis. What is most interesting to us, from the standpoint of civility, is why Palin earned the incivility news frame, but then carried it with apparent neutrality: It is noted a few times in this sample and beyond that Palin—in contrast to McCain—would not discipline her hecklers and chanters, even when offensive. Perhaps it was this unwillingness to speak up as McCain did that intensified journalistic interest in the angry and mean news frame of Palin's crowds: A few dramatic instances, where Palin made pleas for civility, would likely have enabled her to fight the journalistic frame of incivility.

## Civility, Comfort, and Interactivity

Again, whether Palin's crowds were uncivil or not relative to Obama or Biden crowds is unanswerable and lost to history. But Palin became expert over the course of the fall in what journalists call the generation of "red meat" but what we might call the strategic use of incivility. As noted earlier, it is productive to think of civility and incivility as tools. Whether it was planned or not, we have a "good cop, bad cop" team of McCain and Palin. McCain tries briefly in the fall of 2008 to use civility as a weapon, calming particularly offensive audience members. Palin, in contrast, chose incivility as a tool to engage her publics and build an emotional pitch in favor of the Republican ticket.

The notion that civility has an emotional component, noted in Chapter 1, is underscored well by Palin's uses of incivility. She herself is a passionate orator, and encouraged emotion and passion among her crowds as well, showing great appreciation for it. She praised her crowds repeatedly for their intensity of feeling, their cleverness (unique signs, chants, gifts), and their engagement. Her easy way of discussing her personal life (done with real panache during her convention speech) enabled her to be the "real person," garnering the loyalty of many. She exuded a level of comfort with the personal, with herself, and with the emotional exuberance of the crowd that paved the way for displays of incivility by lone—but tolerated—crowd participants. The warmth Palin radiated at her rallies gave them comfort and inspiration, and her interaction with the crowd made her strategic use of incivility highly effective, at least for those who gathered to hear her in person.

A last note on the comparative journalism that we lacked in campaign coverage: There was one exception I located, from John Broder and Julie Bosman's *New York Times* reports on Palin and Democratic vice presidential hopeful Senator Joe Biden, following them in the final hours of the November campaign. In this article, Biden and Palin are compared, and their rally behaviors described, with the journalists noting that Palin attacks Biden freely but Biden will not do the same: He will not "question her qualifications [to hold national office] or mention any of her verbal blunders." Interestingly, Palin assaults Biden's slips, provides the red meat, and undercuts the crowd-rousing ability of Senator Obama:

> Just as Senator Hillary Rodham Clinton of New York did in the primaries, Ms. Palin dismisses Mr. Obama's oratory as "just words," even as she whips crowds into a frenzy with her own remarks. "The rousing speeches of our opponent, they can fill a stadium," Ms. Palin said. "But they cannot keep our country safe. . . ." Her speeches have relied on repetition, especially words like "tough" and "guts" when applied to Mr. McCain.[22]

This balancing act of Palin's, inciting her own crowds and demeaning the popularity of her opponent, was perhaps odd, but not interesting enough to be a theme that journalists found to be deserving of any sustained focus. This apparent contradiction might be of interest. But its absence as a theme is likely a reflection of the qualitative differences between Obama and Palin crowds. Obama's crowds were large, and the sheer size of them was a source of extensive comment from the primary season through the general election campaign. But since the Obama crowds did not quite encourage the incivility frame so common for Palin coverage, they may have appeared as different animals to the media: Palin's crowds seem almost an extension of her own incivility and passion, while Obama's were more distinct from him as speaker. He too was a compelling orator in a large public setting, but one gets the sense from the coverage that Obama can indeed be separated from the people he addressed. For mainstream journalists covering Obama's and Biden's crowds, there seems nothing close to a "group mind"—volatile crowds, subject to a contagion of chants, jeers, and scary behavior.

The coverage of Palin's and Obama's immense crowds has much to do with expectations. By the fall, journalists and viewers had become accustomed to the large numbers Obama drew, but Palin's were new. Her first address to a large, national audience was at the Republican convention, and she had only two months before Election Day to travel the nation and build momentum at rallies. So there was some mystery and lack of predictability, for both candidate and journalists. Could she keep passions running high? Would her use of incivility as a strategic asset remain at the same level, or would there be an acceleration as Election Day approached? These questions hung in the air during September and October 2008. Palin's short track record in national politics had not yet left a discernable pattern, hence the scintillating nature of her every step onto a new stage. She continued to act in unexpected ways long after the campaign, with her bold public statements, her constant "tweeting," and her abrupt midterm resignation as Alaska's governor in July 2009.

## Watching the Palin Crowds

CNN and the *New York Times*, two outlets that strive for evenhandedness (even if this is not always, or even often achieved), and the proudly partisan, pro-McCain-Palin Fox News, are vital to scrutinize, given their audience share and influence on other media. But it was a complex presidential campaign for television and newspaper journalists to cover, and rallies were just one aspect of it. More intense talk about the Palin crowds could be found on the Internet, where scores of popular bloggers analyzed the rallies with a great deal of partisanship and dubious connection to reality, but often real panache and intelligence. Both pro-Palin and anti-Palin bloggers, through posts to various sites, wrote in celebration or with disgust upon seeing the large crowds, in person or on television. The Internet discourse about Palin, often interwoven with video of her rally performances, is too abundant to code or study with conventional social science methods, and such an effort would probably not be a good use of any person's time or energy. Suffice it to say that nearly every possible manner of smart, ridiculous, or obscene banter about the rallies could be found both during and long after the campaign.

The more thoughtful discussion of rallies on the Internet blogs— putting aside the extensions of mainstream newspapers and networks (e.g., Washingtonpost.com or CNN.com)—focused on the words and phrases Palin used. She repeatedly accused Senator Obama of "palling around with terrorists" and called him a "socialist." But an extraordinary number of professional and amateur bloggers paid considerable attention to crowd reactions as well. They debated fiercely, for example, whether someone did in fact yell "Kill him!" referring to Obama, at a Palin rally in Pennsylvania in October.[23] Also very popular on pro-Palin sites were discussions of the "mainstream media" and their inability to capture properly the size and power of the Palin rallies. The experienced print journalist turned Republican blogger Michelle Malkin wrote the following, and she included pictures sent in by readers who were at the rally:

> The same Obamedia cultists in American newsrooms who didn't miss an opportunity to tout The One's ability to draw massive crowds are AWOL when it comes to showing America the massive crowds turning out for McCain-Palin. (Nothing on the front page of the WaPo website; no crowd shots included in the WaPo "Day in Photos" gallery. And, of course, zippo on the front page of the NYT website.) Reader Norman Bercasio attended the big rally in Fairfax, VA today and has posted a beautiful gallery of pics here. A small taste to give you an idea of the rocking scene [photos followed].[24]

Partisans attempting to film rallies contributed extensive commentary about Palin's rallies, like this from Blogger Interrupted, an Obama partisan site:

It's no wonder that the slightest incitement from Sarah Palin or John McCain will turn one of their rallies into a lynch mob. Just talk to the folks who attend.

My camera was rolling for literally seconds before people happily said to me, on camera, that Barack Obama is a terrorist. If I hadn't spent most of my time at the event inside, waiting for the candidates to show up, I could have gotten dozens of these people on tape.

It appears the McCain campaign has either been told to tone it down by the Secret Service, or is toning it down themselves, because [Obama acquaintance Bill Ayers] never came up in the building. Which is good, because if they had invoked Ayers, this crowd, as you will see from the *YouTube*, [*sic*] would have easily gone to the death threats we've heard before, keeping the Secret Service busy for weeks. . . .

I've been doing blog video for a while, and presidential rallies a lot longer. And this is the most strange, ignorant, uninformed, angry, up-to-no-good, and gullible group of people I've ever seen at a political rally.

Ever.[25]

In his highly ranked blog The Daily Dish, Andrew Sullivan—former editor of the *New Republic*—also closely watched the Palin rallies for their character and her performance. A sample:

I was thinking on similar lines, as I watched Palin's Colorado rally last night with greater and greater hathos. The concept of Palin as a marketing tool, as an emblem of pure content-free identity politics, is very powerful. You can see why on paper, [Republican Bill] Kristol loved her, the way he loved the concept of Iraqi liberation. The only trouble is the actual reality: the fact that she has no record to speak of, that what she has is dreadful, that she has no education, that she is a pathological liar, that she is a vicious hater of those unlike her, that she is a McCarthyite sans communism.[26]

Discourse like this, and far more extreme, was abundant in the fall of 2008, but it behooves the student of political communication to evaluate more directly the rallies captured on video, as imperfect as that process may be. Campaign rallies were numerous and dotted the nation, as candidates traveled in a frenzied manner from state to state, from the summer conventions through Election Day. Thankfully, the *Washington Post* tracked many rallies and archived their dates, one useful resource that enables scholars to then retrieve news coverage and amateur videography of the Palin rallies. A look at the many crowds captured on news footage by professional photographers or amateurs posting film to YouTube can give us some sense of the dynamics at the rallies.[27] The Internet offers hundreds (perhaps thousands) of Palin rally videos—full rally coverage and clips of particular segments—and I immersed myself in these, in search of patterns, emphases, and dynamics.

When one watches the scores of hours of Palin footage available, there are patterns in the rallies that echo the themes I introduced earlier in this book. Evident are Palin's strategic use of incivility in her rhetoric and her uncanny ability to create a comfortable environment for people to express themselves, a notion critical to political talk, as we will see most dramatically in Chapter 4. Interactivity and reciprocity are less interesting in a rally setting, as the "call and response" approach to riling a crowd is common and not at all unique to Palin's style. Like most candidates, Palin recognizes the local community and adds regional color in her remarks, introduces local officials, honors service men and women, promises to clean up corruption on Wall Street and in Washington, and so forth. These are time-honored stump speech techniques because they work.

As evidenced by the Palin videos, as well as those of many candidates over the years, interaction, humor, and passion are vital, even when the audience is partisan and ready to adore the speaker. In addition to the conventional techniques of contemporary stump speaking, Palin used key words and phrases that the McCain campaign believed were working for them. Hence, there is much talk in her speeches of being "mavericks" and avoiding "socialist" policies that an Obama administration might bring. McCain and Palin often led rallies together, but Palin handled many of these events herself as the candidates split up to cover more geographic territory. At some rallies, Ohio resident Joe Wurzelbacher (whom McCain and Palin dubbed Joe the Plumber) joined her on stage, as did well-known musicians like country star Hank Williams, Jr. At the majority of large rallies I could locate on video, at least one member of Palin's nuclear family took the stage with her, most often her husband, Todd Palin.

Interactivity and reciprocity, emotional connection to the audience, and the effective rhetorical invocation of family and values made the Palin rallies exciting and engaging, even for the analyst. This was obvious to me, in reviewing the videos, as well as to the journalists who covered Palin throughout the nation. What is most interesting from our perspective of civility and what can excite crowds are two elements in the rallies: incivility as a rhetorical weapon and implications by Palin that Obama is un-American. Both these tools were most apparent in the final week of the campaign, as tensions ran high and the outcome of the election was not easily predicted. While many pre-election polls indicated that Obama led, there was loud talk about the racial dynamic and whether the polls were in fact accurate. Possible underlying racism in the privacy of the voting booth (the so-called Bradley Effect)[28] and the vital role of voter turnout made the election outcome still appear fundamentally unpredictable for most journalists and observers.

The attacks by Palin implying Obama was un-American were part of her stump speech, as well as of comments by McCain/Palin ticket supporters (such as Senator George Voinovich) in the campaign's final weeks. She famously made the following statements, in Clearwater, Florida, on October 6:

"Obama held one of the first meetings of his political career in Bill Ayers's living room, and they've worked together on various projects in Chicago. . . . These are the same guys who think that patriotism is paying higher taxes—remember that's what Joe Biden had said. And"—she paused and sighed—"I am just so fearful that this is not a man who sees America the way you and I see America, as the greatest force for good in the world. I'm afraid this is someone who sees America as 'imperfect enough' to work with a former domestic terrorist who had targeted his own country."[29]

The accusation about un-Americanism was a multidimensional approach, leaning on what Palin believed were Obama's proposed policies based in "socialism," his voting record as she saw it, and most of all, the company Palin believed Obama kept. Frightening key words are helpful in exciting a crowd, as Le Bon noted more than a hundred years ago, and so they became an omnipresent part of the Palin discourse close to Election Day. Joe the Plumber was particularly useful in this regard, since he was not afraid to use dangerous words to describe Obama's approach to public policy.

Key words are efficient, and accusations of being a "socialist," of course, have a lengthy, negative history in the United States. So in using this approach, Palin upheld a tradition. Her use of the word was not innovative or novel, although this did not prevent a vociferous outcry from Obama's campaign and supporters.[30] While the lack of originality does not make Palin's socialism rhetoric uninteresting, it is in keeping with attacks that have been made by right-wing candidates in the United States for a long time. It is an effective "comfort zone" for the right, and Palin is not the last candidate to use this tactic. Subsequently, it has been a drumbeat of sorts by many critical of Obama's economic policies in his first year as president: The word "socialist" to describe Obama has grown among Americans, according to the Pew Research Center for the People and the Press.[31]

Did Palin use civility, or incivility in this case, as a strategic asset? She excelled at it. What seemed most effective in exciting her audiences, particularly in the closing weeks of the campaign, were the ways she paired personal attacks on Obama with a justification for doing so. She claimed, subtly at first then quite boldly as the campaign came to an end, that it was her *right* to assault Obama and his policies—that her approach was *normative*. One aspect of her stump speech was oriented around Joe the Plumber, who, she reports,

> asked Obama: "What is your intention with these tax increases?" And of course, Obama had to—unscripted—be candid, finally, and let him know [that increased taxes were a certainty].[32]

This aspect of her stump speech worked on multiple levels: She keeps Joe the Plumber alive as the working-class representative she and McCain wanted him to be, a class they hoped to attract to their ticket. Potential tax increases are, of course, a "hot button" issue, so are always an excellent worry to underscore at a large rally. And in this brief, efficient fashion, she managed to imply that Obama was also untruthful to citizens, honest only when somehow forced to be, and a slave to his teleprompter. I found this economy of communication throughout Palin's speeches, and the ability to pack insults so densely is very helpful, given the need to fly from location to location and crowd to crowd as quickly as possible.

Palin does not simply criticize but justifies doing so, sometimes as preface to remarks and sometimes immediately following an attack. In Marietta, Ohio, just days before the election, she said, after noting that Senator Obama "has an ideological commitment to higher taxes": "It is not negative campaigning to call someone out on their record." Similarly, in Columbus, Ohio, on the same day, she argued, "It is not mean-spirited . . . to call someone out on their record, their plans, their associations." And in Bowling Green she had asserted, "Someone's got to do it."[33]

This is not a new rhetorical technique—saying something possibly offensive, then framing it as normative, reasonable, and justified. But Palin is very much at ease with this and does it seamlessly. It is, simultaneously, a flippant response to critics who found her too negative and a good fit with her antimedia trope. She often referred to "mainstream media" as misunderstanding her and holding her to unfair standards of politesse in campaigning. Both the attack and the justification of attack work on a few levels and, again, in a tremendously efficient manner.

Governor Palin was a fine exemplar of using incivility in a strategic manner. It most definitely energized her crowds, as is obvious in the scores of rally videos available. Whether the strategy "worked" or not is, of course, another story, and not easily parsed. It remains unclear whether Senator McCain was aided or hurt by Palin's candidacy, and if she did have a significant effect, its nature is difficult to disentangle. Scholars argue over her effect, and over the coming years we will hopefully see analyses that clarify it for us.

Palin employed standard Republican rhetorical campaign techniques, but with a bold, female voice unlike any before it. Without question, her apparent ability to move crowds was most striking to journalists and other election observers, and one wonders why her particular abilities with crowds were so interesting to so many. The answer likely rests in gender and sexual dynamics, still an evolving phenomenon in public life in 2008.

## Women, Sex, and Crowds

The role that women may play in public has been the source of anxiety for a long while, but it was during the Enlightenment that the struggle over their place accelerated. Women of the eighteenth century, years before the French Revolution, shaped the public sphere through participation in salons, achieving influence in the development of art, literature, and philosophy.[34] But this influence was fleeting, and even at the time, most men—elite and common—doubtless would have agreed with Jean Jacques Rousseau that women were talented but best relegated to the domestic sphere. In a series of writings, Rousseau connects vocal public women to the dangerous spectacle of theater, where too many eyes are upon actors, leading to vanity and temptation. As Joan Landes explains in her study of women during the French revolutionary period, Rousseau argues for the cloister of women in the home:

> In contrast to her ancient counterpart's modesty and political silence, she is charged with an excessive use of speech and language. Despite their pleasing talk, "women have flexible tongues." There is always a danger that they will speak nonsense, speak without proper knowledge of a subject as they are wont to do.[35]

Rousseau may have been a fierce critic of women speaking in public, seeing it as a hazard to both speaker and society, but his fears were well entrenched in Western culture, quite in evidence in later centuries. A variety of insightful scholars have documented these same anxieties about women's speech, particularly women speaking in public settings. Among these studies are Mary Ryan's applications of Jürgen Habermas's work to the status and activities of women in nineteenth-century American politics.[36] And there is work by Judy Walkowitz, who demonstrates how women in nineteenth-century London were often symbolic of depravity. Women in public were conflated with sex, and it was the city (the most fraught public space of all) where the prostitute was the "quintessential female figure of the urban scene," an obsession of a worried middle class, of male fantasy, and of pioneers in public health.[37]

Women did begin to speak about politics in public in nineteenth-century America. As scholar Kenneth Cmiel points out, it was not until the 1820s and 1830s that one could find a woman on a speaking platform in a public setting. He notes that feminist and free thinker

Fannie Wright was one of the earliest speakers, and in 1828 she lectured in Cincinnati:

As the New York *Free Enquirer* put it, by speaking in public, Wright had "with ruthless violence broken loose from the restraints of decorum, which draws a circle around the life of a woman." The *Louisville Focus* argued that Wright had "leaped over the boundary of female modesty" and committed an act against nature. The New York *American* claimed that "Wright waived all claims" to courtesy since by speaking in public she "ceased to be a woman" and became, instead, "a female monster."[38]

Women spoke with increasing force and frequency throughout the nineteenth century, on a range of social and political topics well beyond abolition, suffrage, and other critical matters. But their presence as public orators was still fraught with tension well into the twentieth century, and their often-forced silence was central to the ideology of the women's movement of the 1960s and 1970s.

Today we are accustomed to powerful women orators, in government and the private sector, but I would argue that there is still significant anxiety about powerful women's speech in public, an anxiety very much in evidence in responses to Sarah Palin. She herself was (externally, at least) conflicted about the place of women in public during the campaign, despite the moments of great comfort and pride in her balancing act. She often extolled her competencies as governor and her accomplishments, all while standing as a "proud mom" with her husband and four children. Interspersed with these impressive moments of balance, however, were signals of real confusion about the role of women, herself included. Media and supporters were alternately impressed by her outspokenness and a bit unnerved by it, as I discuss subsequently.

Palin has made perplexing statements about whether she is in fact a feminist. She provided numerous statements in recent years about the importance of women in public life and has spoken often about her days as a high school athlete on the basketball courts of her native Alaska (her days as "Sarah Barracuda"). Yet during the presidential election campaign of 2008, Palin was asked about feminism directly and expressed conflicting views, as noted by Bonnie Erbe of *U.S. News and World Report*:

> In an interview on NBC Nightly News that aired yesterday, Brian Williams asked Palin: "Governor, are you a feminist?"
>
> "I'm not gonna label myself anything, Brian," said Palin. "And I think that's what annoys a lot of Americans, especially in a political campaign, is to start trying to label different parts of America different, different backgrounds, different. . . . I'm not going to put a label on myself."
>
> But label herself is just what she did last month in an interview with CBS's Katie Couric, who asked her if she considered herself a feminist. Her answer was an unabashed, "I do."[39]

It is not clear why Palin is inconsistent on an issue on which one might expect her to have a somewhat more crystallized response. There are multiple possibilities: She had not thought about it much previously, was inexperienced in the ways of message consistency, was naively attempting to have it both ways and appeal to multiple audiences, or is in fact deeply conflicted about the matter. At one of the strangest Palin rally moments—in Carson, California—she commented on a Madeline Albright quote that she noticed on her disposable Starbucks coffee cup:

> I'm reading on my Starbucks mocha cup, okay? The quote of the day . . . [i]t was Madeleine Albright, former Secretary of State [crowd boos] and UN ambassador. . . . Now she said it, I didn't. She said, "There's a place in Hell reserved for women who don't support other women."
>
> [Crowd cheers]

Okay, now, thank you so much for receiving that well.
I didn't know how that was gonna go over. And now, California, let's see what a comment like I just made, how that is
turned into whatever it'll be turned into tomorrow with the
newspaper.[40]

This rally occurred on October 4, approximately midway between Palin's nomination and Election Day. At that point in the
campaign, there was still some talk of her possible capture of Hillary
Clinton loyalists (Clinton having lost to Obama in the Democratic
primaries that spring). The Albright quip was not repeated—at least
in publically available recorded rallies—and did not become part of
her stump speech. It appeared to be spontaneous, something she had
not reflected on for very long. She seemed to be arguing that gender
trumps party affiliation, and this argument coheres with the comments about "glass ceilings" that she made often through the campaign, in pursuit of disappointed Hillary Clinton voters. It was a trial
balloon, as she notes, an attempt to see how a strong female statement
might work in her rally situations. Was she asking their permission
to be a feminist? She developed such intimacy and warmth with her
crowds that approval-seeking behavior was a fit with the supportive
atmosphere. Again, she makes a somewhat harsh remark, then adds a
comment about how her remark will likely be distorted by journalists,
consistent with her chronic, straightforward focus on how she will appear in media. Here, the Palin crowd is both supporter and arbiter.

While Palin was, in public at least, conflicted on the subject of
her own feminism, journalists seemed less interested in her beliefs
about women elected officials or women's issues more generally. Apart
from the network interviews I have cited, it is not a common theme
in coverage of Palin's campaign, certainly not of her rallies. Occasionally columnists raised the question, particularly Maureen Dowd,
her harsh critic at the *New York Times*, who—among other names—
called Palin "Caribou Barbie." But on the whole, the media seemed far
more interested in her appearance—clothing, shoes, hair, and overall

sex appeal. These items, in contrast to philosophical or practical discussions of feminism, were of tremendous interest to journalists, in fact, and became prominent well before accusations of her spending Republican donors' funds on clothes came to dominate the news.[41]

As she stepped into the national spotlight, there was much chatter on Internet sites, in blogs, and in the conventional media about Palin's physical attributes as soon. There was pervasive talk about her "good looks" or "youth" (often a code word for female beauty) and much about her sexual appeal to male voters. An unusual article on a Palin event, for a leading news outlet—unique in its length and sustained attention to sex—was by Mark Leibovich of the *New York Times*, who followed Palin on the campaign trail in mid-October. He notes that Palin's popularity rate upon the announcement of her candidacy in early fall was higher among men than women (although it would later drop). At rallies, he notes, men were engaged and taken with Palin's attractiveness, physical as well as ideological. One Indiana man sported a "Proud to be voting for a hot chick" Palin campaign button. Leibovich notes:

> While there are plenty of women, including wives and daughters of male fans, at Ms. Palin's appearances, they acknowledge they are outnumbered. "This is not a ladies campaign," declared Linda Teegan at a rally in Weirs Beach, N.H., on Wednesday. She was taking a crowd snapshot. "There seem to be lots and lots of guys here," she said. "I'd guess 70–30, maybe 65–35, men to women. It's quite noticeable to me." . . . "You tell 'em baby," a man yelled out [to Palin] at a rally Wednesday night on a high school football field in Salem, N.H.

He continues:

> Yes, some men come to ogle the candidate, too. "She's beautiful," said a man wearing a John Deere T-shirt in Weirs Beach. "I came here to look at her."[42]

This sort of commentary about an attractive woman is, of course, pervasive throughout American mass media, and so comports well with a general social obsession with younger, attractive women.[43] And we have long, perhaps beginning in earnest with Jackie Kennedy, examined all aspects of prominent women's physical features in the highest strata of American politics. But the intensity of focus on Palin was still unusual, since it fit so neatly into the cultural framing of women in public noted by nineteenth-century historians. Female presence in public space has the potential to sexualize that space, making it a place to act out the gender and sexual dynamics of a larger society. In nineteenth-century London, the prostitute was the public woman in an urban setting, and during just the same era in the American Midwest, social reformer Fannie Wright was called an immodest "female monster" who had in fact ceased to be truly female because of her speech making.

Palin was called a monster, typically in left-leaning publications, and it is fascinating how far the "sexy danger" theme went, and so quickly after her nomination. In one Salon essay, Palin is caricatured as a dominatrix, with the article subtitle noting, "Sarah Palin is trying to seduce independent voters. But she comes across like a whip-wielding mistress who wants to discipline a naughty America." It continues:

> Because Palin's a woman, and even more, a babe, suddenly she and her party have been magically transformed into fresh-faced reformers. Like Kafka's "Metamorphosis" in reverse, the giant, hideous beetle that was the GOP has suddenly been reborn as a vigorous youth—one that even claims to be a "maverick."[44]

Blatant sexual appeal and its powerful, mysterious role seemed omnipresent in journalistic discourse, if often more subtle than Leibovich described from his travels with Palin. As social historians note, sex and danger have been conflated: Women speaking boldly in public are both attractive and frightening. They turn the world upside down even now, when attractive women on the attack are still a rarity in American presidential campaigns in the early twenty-first century. Palin may have been seen as "dangerous" for her ideas, her personal attacks on opponents, and other aspects of her rhetoric. But underlying this surface danger is a specifically female sort of menace, and Palin was a fulcrum for this multiplicity of variables: She seemed, consciously or unconsciously, to be a tableau for a society still working through their comfort with women in public. From Fannie Wright, to Eleanor Roosevelt, to Barbara Jordan, to Hillary Clinton and Sarah Palin, the two-pronged danger (ideas plus sex) is a fascinating thread still running through American politics. Its character changes with the woman in question, given how few emerge at the highest levels, but Palin demonstrates that women in public are still a tremendous source of wonder and social anxiety.

## Palin and Clinton

One might argue that Palin simply inherits the blows—albeit in a somewhat different style—that Hillary Clinton has suffered for quite a while, since she appeared with her husband as a political figure in Arkansas in the 1970s. From her days as a target of wonder and harsh criticism in Arkansas (women graduates of Yale Law School were not very common as political spouses), through the trials of President Bill Clinton's infidelities in the 1990s, and through the grueling primary against Barack Obama, Hillary Clinton stands in a quite well documented class by herself in the realm of gender and politics study.

Perhaps the gendered assaults on Palin were a modified version of those on Clinton, with a few new twists? Absolutely; there is a clear pattern of critique against women with a lengthy history, as noted previously. But what makes the Palin case equally fascinating, and not a simple repeat of American gender discrimination, is that she defied the comfortable analytic categories Clinton represented: Palin did not call herself a feminist with ease or pride, was not a student activist or spokesperson in the 1960s, stole "glass ceiling" language from Clinton, and unlike Clinton, had no long history of work on behalf of women and children. Clinton was an Ivy League graduate, an easy lightning rod for America's fierce decades-long struggle with womanhood, work, and motherhood. Palin, by contrast, *is* a conservative—coming from the very part of the ideological continuum that found Clinton so worrisome for so long. The attacks on Palin were vicious but in a somewhat more complex fashion than Clinton's have long been: Liberal bloggers and commentators were intent on demeaning Palin, but they walked a difficult tightrope, often revealing as many misogynistic tendencies as conservatives have displayed in dealing with Clinton's talents.

It is not my intention to argue that Sarah Palin is the first woman figure to be castigated or treated poorly, far from it. And I certainly cannot argue that she suffered more than the public women who withstood decades of critique and abuse, like Eleanor Roosevelt or Hillary Clinton. The treatment of Palin is consistent with the female discrimination of recent decades, but she has not lived it very long at all. My point is that she represents *the fusion of gender politics and the complexities of civility in our time.* Like both Roosevelt and Clinton, Palin was treated in ways that were certainly uncivil. But she used incivility to her own strategic advantage as well—in ways that Clinton never did. Palin developed unique modes of (for lack of a better phrase) "strong woman incivility" the likes of which we do not see very often at all. Her rallies were unusual, her rhetoric was unique, and her impact on the American scene was tremendous as a result. She is the conservative woman politician many on the right awaited, but did not realize they awaited until she appeared with vigor at the Republican convention. And Palin is an unexpected mix of highly feminine strength and conservative values that threw her opponents and journalists out of their normal patterns of expectation.

A last note on Clinton: Didn't she attack as well, during the brutal primary against Obama? What of her attack ads and Internet videos, the proxies used to bring down Obama, and the constant assaults on

Obama's inexperience by both Clinton and her husband? Of course, there was negative campaigning from the Clinton camp, and this is well documented. But there is a clear difference between attacks on one's record (votes cast, positions taken) or lack of record (Obama's lack of executive experience, his "present" votes in the Illinois legislature) and using incivility as a strategic weapon. Some observers of the Clinton campaign felt that President Clinton raised the issue of race—to turn whites against Obama—and that Clinton did so herself: In New Hampshire, for example, her remarks about Lyndon Johnson being essential to transforming Martin Luther King's dreams into legislative action were seen by some as belittling King.[45] But in general, the Clinton campaign and Clinton herself refrained from the type of incivility Palin engaged in—linking Obama with a "terrorist," calling him a socialist, and so forth. The nature of the language Palin used was in an entirely different category from Clinton's or even her more virulent proxies. Palin is interesting to us for her gender—and all the disadvantages that entails—as well as her strategic use of both civility (warmth, the toting of children to events) and incivility.

———

Sarah Palin resigned as Alaska Governor in July 2009, eighteen months before the end of her first term. Just before the July Fourth holiday weekend, she held a press conference to explain her reasons, emphasizing the toll that ethics complaints and personal assaults had taken on both the state of Alaska and her family. The resignation was, and still is, as of this writing, of great interest to journalists, pundits, elected officials, political party leaders, and citizens on all parts of the ideological spectrum. Her future in American politics and culture is unclear, but there is no question that her presence is a powerful one.

For our purposes, Palin is a case study in the strategic use of incivility. This is not to say that she was a monster, as claimed by many, or that her rhetoric is unacceptable by a strict standard of political civility, since we do not have one. As I have noted, stated standards of civility are not particularly useful to the analyst, given their fluctuation and context-specific nature. But if civility and incivility are best seen as weapons, Palin presents an instructive case, made even more interesting by her status as the first Republican woman vice presidential candidate.

Beyond the strategic use of incivility, however, Palin reflects characteristics of tremendous civility as well, and we need to keep this point in the analytic mix. She engaged audiences, particularly at rallies, with warmth and gratitude. Her interaction with her crowds—and they were very much hers—was highly dialogic in both the conventional shout-out fashion of American campaigning and in a more specialized persuasion of sorts. All this was noted, if often in a clunky and unsophisticated manner, by conventional media outlets. What they missed was that her technique ran to the heart of how civility and incivility are both thoroughly and self-reflexively *tactical*, thrown on and off, in an age of constant media attention and Internet chatter. We shall see more of this in campaigns of the future, as we continue to struggle with the bounds of negativity and incivility in our workplaces, in our neighborhoods, and in our Internet interactions.

# 3 / Barack Obama,
# Difference, and Civility

I n the spring of 2009, the newly elected American president planned to accept an honorary doctor of laws degree from the University of Notre Dame. The 167-year-old university had conferred this honor on nine previous presidents of the United States, and President Barack Obama prepared to go to South Bend, Indiana, to deliver the commencement address and collect the degree. But given his stated positions—support of abortion rights and stem cell research—controversy erupted among students, alumni, and others over whether the storied Catholic institution should bestow honors on President Obama.

In the end, amid loud and somewhat disruptive outrage on the part of some students, alumni, and friends of the university, Obama gave his speech and in it took on the issue of abortion directly. But he also used the opportunity to discuss tolerance, civility, and political discourse. He used civility (humor, warmth, interactivity with the audience)—as well as metalevel talk about the nature of civility—as a strategy to calm the storms surrounding the speech. Most interesting for the discussions in this book was his attempt to forge a philosophy about difficult political talk in the United States about abortion, and how we might locate civility in this most passionate and hurtful of cultural debates.

Several months after Obama spoke about civility at Notre Dame, he was confronted with a far weightier and more intense controversy: the debate over the future of American health care. Interestingly, between the commencement speech in May and the discussion of civility in the "town meetings" in the summer and fall of 2009, Obama, his opponents, the mass media, and the public all turned toward civility—as an idea—and the nature of discourse. This shift was not planned, and it was certainly an annoyance to many trying to pursue complex policy change. While the health care debate continues at this writing, the nature of civility in town meetings across the nation is of tremendous value in understanding political talk in our time. The behavior in the town meetings, together with media coverage of them, fits squarely into our discussion of incivility as a strategic weapon, the nature of emotional comfort in politics, and the impact of new media on public debate.

But we begin with events leading up to the Notre Dame speech and the speech itself, in an attempt to understand one president's inchoate views on civility. It is not possible to determine the effects of the speech: At the time, graduates and their families seemed appreciative and respectful, as did many in the news media. Others had been appalled by the invitation and were unconvinced by the speech. It is not my goal to pass judgment on the effect of the speech, as we lack the tools to disentangle this rhetorical moment from all the other speeches and actions of the president that spring. But the speech is very much worth our keen attention as the first formal statement—in a public, highly fraught setting—of a president who built so much of his campaign and narrative of self around difference, tolerance, and civility. It may go down in history as a minor speech, a vitally important and successful one, or a shining moment in what becomes a failed presidency. Time will tell, but I argue here that it foreshadows Obama's communicative stance on controversial issues to come. His performance at Notre Dame provides some clues as to how he sees the American public as well. All the while—as he constitutes *a public* and defines political reality—he leans hard on the notion of civil discourse.

The speech should be seen as a shot over the bow—a young president with strong, evolving notions of civility trying to find his voice and his way. For that reason, regardless of its immediate value or impact for Americans, it is a historical document of possibly great significance.

## Presidents on "Civility"

Very few U.S. presidents have addressed civility (or difficult political discourse) directly, a lack which is surprising, given the power of the word in democratic history. A search of the archives of the American Presidency Project, which includes over 86,000 documents and speeches (formal and informal) from President George Washington to Barack Obama, yields only 129 mentions of "civility" by presidents. And nearly all mention it in passing, as a word on a list with other keywords (e.g., decency or humility in a Jimmy Carter speech).[1] This is not to say that previous presidents did not recognize the nature of our political divides and did not struggle with them. But they did not often do so in public.

Of the 129 mentions of civility, there is only one before 1961—John Adams's special message to the House of Representatives. In a brief note to Congress, about interaction with Great Britain on the high seas, Adams noted in 1799:

It is but justice to say that this is the first instance of misbehavior of any of the British officers toward our vessels of war that has come to my knowledge. According to all the representations that I have seen, the flag of the United States and their officers and men have been treated by the civil and military authority of the British nation in Nova Scotia, the West India islands, and on the ocean with uniform civility, politeness, and friendship. I have no doubt that this first instance of misconduct will be readily corrected.[2]

After this use of the word, it does not appear again until President John F. Kennedy used it in his inaugural address, speaking of the Cold War and his hope for peace among nations:

> So let us begin anew—remembering on both sides that civility is not a sign of weakness, and sincerity is always subject to proof. Let us never negotiate out of fear. But let us never fear to negotiate.[3]

The lengthy historical gap in the use of the word "civility" is fascinating, since it was in common use and is employed without a fuss in the Adams message. The uses of the word from Kennedy up to Obama's Notre Dame speech are not quite worthy of analysis, as the word is mentioned in passing and is not a central focus of the presidents. But it is important to note that every leader after Kennedy did use the word, and sometimes often (President Bill Clinton used it 45 times and President George W. Bush 24 times). Perhaps this frequency of use is due to the overarching concerns about civility in the United States that were recognized with great anxiety from the 1960s on—the violence surrounding the civil rights and student movements, increasing crime in our cities, and a sense that manners have been in a linear decline. In any case, in 2009, civility mattered enough for a president to make it the central theme of an early, highly anticipated public address.

## The End of a Campaign and the Start of a Presidency

In May 2009, President Obama was popular, as documented by presidential approval ratings collected by the Gallup organization. Good ratings are expected for presidents early in their first terms, and Obama's figures looked very much like those of previous presidents, no matter how small or large their margins of election victory.[4] In the second quarter, from April to July, presidents ranged from a high of 76 percent approval (Kennedy) to 44 percent (Clinton). Obama's average approval statistic during this period was 62 percent, similar to where Richard Nixon, Carter, Ronald Reagan, and George H. W. Bush stood. When he gave his Notre Dame speech in May, Obama was in a strong position, with most Americans optimistic about their president.

A newly elected president's early speeches often reflect the campaign just ended, and this was certainly true of Obama. Even into July 2009, Obama referenced the hard-fought general election campaign of 2008 and used many phrases from campaign discourse. The Notre Dame speech seems in part an extension of campaign ideas, and one of Obama's books on public policy—published during the campaign—is cited during the speech. So we should treat a May 2009 speech as a persuasive appeal very much in the spirit of the campaign rhetoric it echoed. It was not a speech of brand new ideas, but any words spoken during a campaign take on a very different meaning when delivered by a sitting president, no matter how common or even tired they felt during a long campaign. I think of the Notre Dame address as a hybrid of leadership speech genres, difficult to place in any category. It is not a campaign-type speech, desperate to move voters. But it does not consistently use the more confident, authoritative tone presidents employ further into their terms.

There is a vast literature on presidential speeches, and it is enormously helpful to us, even if the Notre Dame speech is idiosyncratic in many ways. Leading scholars on the topic include giants like Kathleen Hall Jamieson, George Edwards, and Jeffrey Tulis, pioneers who have traced presidential speech over time, characterized how it has changed, and, best of all, opened new questions that students of the presidency have explored and debated continuously for two decades.[5] It is not my intention here to review these debates, but they have been vital, underscoring how and why presidents use the "bully pulpit" to achieve their national policy goals. The important function of presidential speech is to shape audiences, and indeed nations. Campbell and Jamieson put it well, noting that presidents invite us to be a people:

> When we say that presidents constitute the people, we mean that all presidents have the opportunity to persuade us to conceive of ourselves in ways compatible with their views of government and the world. At the same time, presidents invite us to see them, the presidency, the country, and the country's roles in specific ways.[6]

This approach is a general guide to understanding what presidents are often trying to do in their speeches, whether an inaugural or an address to a particular audience, given that nearly all contemporary presidential public events are captured on video. Presidents often address an audience of millions no matter how small the venue for their actual speech, and their remarks are preserved on the Internet for all to see for the indeterminate future. Obama chose, at a moment of goodwill with regard to national approval ratings, to broach the topic of civility, and through his speech we might be able to detect what sort of American public he thinks we are and wants us to become. In this case, civility is a preface as he tries to define his vision, and he also—without intending to—broaches the enduring question about what public opinion actually is. But we must acknowledge first that all speeches are tied to their settings; the preamble in this case, a controversy among opponents of abortion rights, matters immensely. And the particularities of commencement addresses in general matter as well. What was the president "walking into," exactly, before he was able to deliver the speech?

## A Contentious Invitation

Notre Dame has hosted many presidents, and inviting the newly elected president both to receive an honorary degree and to deliver a commencement speech was in keeping with their tradition as a leading national university. Many colleges and universities compete for high-profile leaders to anoint their graduates each spring, and to get the president of the United States is a mighty coup. In the spring of 2009, the president attended only two other commencements, at the United States Naval Academy and at Arizona State University.[7]

Many in both the on-campus and external Notre Dame communities supported the university's decision to invite President Obama and hear him speak. Some students and administrators argued that support for these decisions was strong, with one campus center director claiming, "The majority of students and faculty are really thrilled and honored. . . . It doesn't have a feel that it's splitting the campus."[8] Indeed, President Obama had won a mock presidential election on campus the previous fall, beating Senator John McCain by more than 10 percent of those participating.[9] Externally, a survey conducted by the Pew Forum found that most Catholics who followed the Notre Dame controversy over Obama supported the university decision, with 50 percent believing it was right to invite him and 25 percent opposing it. The total U.S. population favored the decision by more than 20 percentage points.[10]

Despite these statistics, many Notre Dame students and alumni vehemently opposed the grant of an honorary degree and spoke about it on campus, to the media, and in a variety of other forums. An online opposition petition garnered more than 64,000 signers, decrying Obama's positions "that directly contradict fundamental Catholic teaching on life and marriage." The Cardinal Newman Society stated on their Web site:

> Notre Dame has chosen prestige over principles, popularity over morality. . . . Whatever may be President Obama's admirable qualities, this honor comes on the heels of some of the most anti-life actions of any American president, including expanding federal funding for abortions and inviting taxpayer-funded research on stem cells from human embryos.[11]

Many student, faculty, and alumni opponents made special efforts to distinguish their dislike of Obama's positions on abortion and stem cell research from other aspects of the man and his presidency. But many others did not, seeing these issues as central to this president's worldview and dangerous for American public policy into the future.

Despite the controversy, Obama came to Notre Dame and gave his speech as planned. He fulfilled the goal of the best commencement addresses by taking on a big theme with passion. The audience was respectful and appreciative, although there was a student/community demonstration outside the commencement venue, some graduating seniors who chose not to attend their own commencement, and an audience member who yelled, "Abortion is murder. Stop killing children." The heckler was removed, and the audience booed and chanted in support of Obama's attempt to continue speaking. Obama proceeded to acknowledge the heckler and audience, and cited the Notre Dame valedictorian, who said, "We don't do things easily." After initial jokes about athletics, the economy, climate change, and the challenges to this generation of graduates, Obama turned to his central issues, conflict of beliefs and abortion.[12]

## Constituting a Civil Public around Abortion

If presidents typically invite us to become "the people" they hope for, Obama does much the same at Notre Dame. He asks that Americans be guided by civility, no matter their differences, and he does so through a variety of classical rhetorical techniques. One common one, used by compelling rhetoricians, is to associate oneself with a person the audience regards highly. Obama does so by mentioning his work as a community organizer in Chicago, in partnership with the local Catholic Church and the late archbishop of Chicago, Cardinal Bernardin. And he uses humor and self-mockery throughout the speech, noting, for example, that he was "really broke and [the church folks] fed me." Then there are multiple appeals in the tripartite Aristotelian tradition, as Obama appeals to the audience's emotions (pathos), to logic (logos), and to his own character or ethos, specifically, his own strong religious faith.

With regard to the nature of presidential discourse, rhetoric scholar David Zarefsky provides a concise, although not comprehensive, set of tools to evaluate a leader's speech across genres. Zarefsky argues that rhetoric is situational, and, of course, no two presidential speeches are alike in form or effect. However "patterns of rhetorical choice" can be located across speech situations, and so should be studied like great literature, trying to understand the specific instance (speaker, text, and audience) while at the same time contributing insights about presidential speech more generally. Zarefsky argues that presidents work to define social situations and political reality, in strategic attempts to make empirical facts work in their favor and persuade publics. He notes:

> The definition of the situation affects what counts as data for or against a proposal, highlights certain elements of the situation for use in arguments and obscures others, influences whether people will notice the situation and how they will handle it, describes causes and identifies remedies, and invites moral judgments about circumstances or individuals. Accordingly, presidential definition resembles what William Riker calls heresthetic: "The art of structuring the world so you can win."[13]

Zarefsky notes four techniques presidents have used to define political reality, their opponents, and their proposals, and all are useful to us in evaluating Obama's speech on civility. The first is to link terms by forcing associations among them, something close to providing new analogies for understanding a situation. In Obama's speech, he tries to redefine the debate about abortion through multiple attempts at reassociation. While many pro-life activists have focused on what they believe is murder of an innocent life, and pro-choice advocates emphasize a woman's right to choose, Obama asks that we set our sights on reducing the number of abortions and supporting pregnant women. While obviously not what either side in the debate seeks as an ultimate solution, this approach does provide another way to view the realities of unintended pregnancy, and neither group of advocates can argue with it. Here the president provides a new association for the notion of abortion (abortion should be thought of in tandem with pregnancy prevention and reduction), hoping to make this linkage stick in political discourse.

Another tool at a president's disposal is "dissociation," which Zarefsky describes as "breaking a concept into parts in order to identify one's proposal with the more favored part. One prefers the spirit of the law over the letter, the real over the apparent, practice over theory, and so on."[14] In the Notre Dame speech, Obama practices dissociation subtly, by trying to take apart the components of the phenomenon that is an abortion, dividing it into (1) the decision, and then (2) the action (either taking the fetus to term or destroying it). Obama argues:

> When we open up our hearts and our minds to those who may not think precisely like we do or believe precisely what we believe—that's when we discover at least the possibility of common ground. That's when we begin to say, "Maybe we won't agree on abortion, but we can still agree that this heart-wrenching decision for any woman is not made casually, it has both moral and spiritual dimensions."

By expanding abortion into a longer chain of events over time, even if the time is only a matter of difficult days, then parsing it into a hard decision plus an action, he redefines the essence of the experience. The event is elongated and then split, and this seems an effective way to disassociate abortion from "killing," the most treacherous aspect of the debate from the perspectives of both sides.

A third technique is the time-honored attempt to create a symbol—a "condensation symbol"—that efficiently combines and indeed shrinks diverse meanings of an issue. If one can create a symbol or theme, one might channel emotion or conflict into something useful in persuasion. Examples abound in presidential rhetoric, from Roosevelt's "new deal" to Reagan's "welfare queens" to Bush's "war on terror." In the Obama speech, he turns to these condensation symbols: "Open hearts. Open minds. Fair-minded words." These are interesting turns of phrase for us, because they are simultaneously attempts to find middle ground on abortion and key elements of civility. Through these three concepts, strung together, he appeals to pathos and logos, emotion and logic, while also pointing to talk itself as something that will save us from our conflicted selves. He "invites" (in Campbell and Jamieson's sense) the American public, his audience, to be the sort of people who can string these notions together. It is a highly ambitious proposition, and fundamental to at least some conceptions of participatory democracy.

Two other condensation symbols are borrowed by Obama from Father Theodore Hesburgh, renowned former president of Notre Dame (he was in the audience), who argued that the institution was "a lighthouse and a crossroads": It sheds wisdom for Catholics and their belief systems, but is also a place where people with differences can debate each other, with respect and even love. Obama comes back to these two symbols later in the speech, as they are powerful ways to express his own belief in passionate feeling and passionate debate. How one balances these ideals is, of course, a difficult matter, but they seem to be effective symbols that gather up some very tough issues in a neat package, used strategically by the president.

Finally, although there are scores of other intriguing aspects of the speech for students of political communication, of particular note here is Obama's effort to engage in "frame shifting," where leaders shine new light on a situation, in hopes of redefining it in their favor. Zarefsky argues that George W. Bush employed the framing technique on foreign policy:

> President Bush employed frame shifting in his *ex post facto*
> justification for the 2003 war in Iraq. When no weapons of

mass destruction were found, he invited listeners to see the war from the perspective of the benefits of eliminating a tyrant, even though that had not been the original justification, rather than from the frame of protecting the United States and other nations against the risk of biological, chemical, or nuclear weapons.[15]

Obama engages in frame shifting throughout the speech, but most importantly for our purposes tries to reorient the entire abortion debate to a search for civility. He addresses abortion fully, but he mentions other parties and issues that also involve great conflict in American politics—stem cell research, for example. While he does not put it quite this baldly, he asks the public to revisit how they talk about difficult issues and to mend what he sees as the problematic nature of civil discourse. He asks a variety of questions, among them, "As citizens of a vibrant and varied democracy, how do we engage in vigorous debate?"

## Models of Public Opinion and Civility

Obama argues in the speech that pro-choice and pro-life advocates may never agree. He says, "No matter how much we may want to fudge it—indeed, while we know that the views of most Americans on the subject are complex and even contradictory—the fact is that at some level, the views of the two camps are irreconcilable." This is an intriguing aspect of the speech, possibly revealing how Obama sees public opinion more generally: Is there actually one American public, or is it a conglomeration of groups, often divided and in opposition to each other? I would argue that, although it is an early moment in the Obama presidency and leaders shift and change in their views of public opinion, this president's views cohere with the wing of public opinion theory represented best by Arthur Bentley and Herbert Blumer. Both saw public opinion not as an aggregate of individuals opining to pollsters who add up their views, but as an *arena* for the clash of group passions and ideas. Neither Bentley, writing in the first decade of the twentieth century, or Blumer, writing in the 1940s and 1950s, was overly cynical about the nature of American politics. Their ideas, while certainly coming from a critical point of view, sprang from a view that public opinion is a battlefield of sorts, and a sociological framework is the only one that helps us to understand the empirical reality.

Bentley's most famous work is *The Process of Government*, published in 1908 and largely overlooked by students of American politics. Bentley covered a variety of topics, but he was particularly enamored with the activities of interest groups and how they shape public opinion dynamics. He wrote:

> Just as one can nowhere find a "social whole" as a factor in society, so one can nowhere find a unanimous public opinion which is the opinion of the whole society, of every member of it. There will be group arrayed against group and opinion group against opinion group.[16]

In this view, public opinion is a sort of rhetorical public space as much as it is a dynamic attitudinal phenomenon. His is a highly sociological view, and Bentley spends much of his time arguing that groups have organization and interests, and that to ignore these in the study of American public opinion is to not study it at all. While this view of public opinion did not stick, and in fact the study of interest groups and the study of public opinion are now two distinct and largely unconnected scholarly fields, it remains powerful and omnipresent nonetheless. When our leaders think about public opinion, they are far less likely to think about polls—especially now, given the multiplicity of outlets for expression of public opinion—than about interest groups and how they clash. The 2009 national debate about health care reform is probably the most obvious high-profile clash, where group interests are well understood and the president tries to navigate, cajole, and compromise with them. This clash of opposing group interests is then reflected in the fight to characterize public opinion—what people want from their medical care, how much they are willing to spend, how rich insurance companies can become, and whether taxing wealthier citizens is an acceptable route to universal coverage.

Bentley tried to tie the study of public opinion dynamics to the clashes of vocal, organized groups, and Blumer picked up on this approach years later with increased sophistication and fervor.[17] He saw public opinion as a battle of group interests, very much tied to power hierarchies, and thought of the public as an organic, dynamic entity: The public is as complex as the innards of an animal, and to understand that animal, one must try to examine it in its entirety. In his most famous essay on the topic, Blumer was arguing directly against the then-new public opinion survey, which had become influential in his field of sociology. His goal was to persuade all social scientists to reject the notion that a survey, no matter how scientifically and carefully conducted, truly samples a moment in time. He also argued that the real nature of public opinion cannot be represented by sampled individuals, people who are anonymously polled and never know each other or act together in society. Blumer saw surveyors as doing useful work but not approaching public opinion in the least. While Blumer and Bentley both regard public opinion as an organic entity, reflected in part by the clash of powerful interests— their view did not dominate the field. Far from it, survey research blossomed in both academe and industry, and both scholars are seen as cranky dinosaurs, to be ignored in a steady climb to more polling and surveying.

While it is notoriously difficult to know how much any sitting president or his administration relies on opinion polls for policy guidance or on framing issues, given other influences on them (e.g., Congress, nightly news broadcasts, Internet chatter), the Obama White House, like all others, no doubt monitors polls with great interest. At the least, since polls can be just looked at for their news value on a particular day, Obama is arguing implicitly that public opinion is a conflicted, moving target. On this point, he uses some of the strongest language in the speech, noting that common ground is very hard to find on many issues:

And part of the problem, of course, lies in the imperfections of man—our selfishness, our pride, our stubbornness,
our acquisitiveness, our insecurities, our egos; all the cruelties large and small that those of us in the Christian tradition
understand to be rooted in original sin. We too often seek
advantage over others. We cling to outworn prejudice and
fear those who are unfamiliar. Too many of us view life only
through the lens of immediate self-interest and crass materialism; in which the world is necessarily a zero-sum game.

While Obama, both before and after this section of the speech,
returns to his hopes for common ground, he acknowledges here that
the public and public opinion are rife with conflict. In fact, the clash
of interests seems a driver, a force that shapes political life and the
daily lives of all Americans. His preferred cause is biblical (original
sin) but cause matters not in this view of human nature. While neither Bentley nor Blumer wrote of public opinion from the standpoint
of spirituality or brotherhood, they saw the public sphere in much the
same way. It is in the clashes themselves that we see the fundamental challenge of American political debate, and it is here that we learn
the most about the dynamics of public opinion on difficult matters.
Particularly interesting is Obama's reference to a "zero-sum game,"
that there are winners and losers in American political debates. He
goes on to say that a college education—one such as the Notre Dame
graduates had received—will enable people to figure out how to be
civil, even when both people and the world they have created are so
deeply flawed.

## Health Care, Town Meetings, and the President

The Notre Dame speech foreshadowed what would follow for President Obama a few months later: Civility would become one of the
most important themes in American public discourse. Obama was as
prepared as most presidents can be for a raucous, unpredictable pub-

lic debate. But there is no question that the health care reform debate of 2009 forced the president to think harder about civility and talk more about it as well.

During the 2008 presidential election campaign, then-Senator Obama and his Republican opponent, Senator John McCain, both spoke about the importance of health care reform. It was the focus of presidential debates and was repeatedly addressed in meetings across the nation. The challenges presented by tens of millions of uninsured citizens were central to the conversation, as were the increasing costs of health insurance for average Americans and businesses alike. The fact that health care costs play such a dominant role in the larger national economy drove the discussion as well, although it seemed a bit theoretical relative to the "real people" with problems in political advertisements and at rallies (e.g., those who lost coverage when they were laid off, or people rejected by insurers for preexisting conditions). While the candidates debated the issues and traded barbs, they both saw reform as vital, given the macrolevel effects of health care on the economy over the long term.

McCain went back to the Senate after his loss, and the president, good to his campaign promises, approached health care with vigor in the spring of 2009. Along with pulling the nation out of a recession, the need to gain energy independence, and other priorities, health care became a dominant stream in his speeches and interviews. As presidents often do, he expressed his strong preferences but allowed that Congress would need to debate and pursue legislation. He and his staff were in constant discussion with leading legislators of both parties, but despite their efforts Obama did not see legislation before the August 2009 congressional recess, and he was resigned to using the recess as a time for national discussion. He encouraged legislators to hold "town hall meetings" to bring the issues to their constituents back home and listen to public opinion. He held town meetings himself, although as president, his were highly regulated national showcases, far beyond his experiences during his days as a legislator in Illinois.

Senators and representatives in great numbers did return home in August and did hold town hall meetings. These ranged from the calm and intellectual to the raucous and entirely out of control. It is impossible to count the number of town meetings held during that late summer period, but there were hundreds, led by and starring legislators themselves.

"Town hall meeting" (or simply "town meeting") is a wonderful phrase, of course, encapsulating the direct democracy lauded by Alexis de Tocqueville and other visitors to a young, nineteenth-century American democracy. Before the health care debates of 2009, I would argue, "town meeting" connoted rational, community discourse of the most impressive sort. Perhaps this connotation was reinforced (regardless of what town meetings have actually been like in the United States) by Norman Rockwell's famous painting of a working-class man, with grit under his fingernails, standing up to say his piece in the 1943 painting *Freedom of Speech*.

Traditionally, town meetings have been associated with regular hearings, held by local bodies, like school boards, city councils, or zoning boards. A mayor might call a special town meeting on a topic that has suddenly attracted interest as well, and those are very often the ones best attended in a community—a meeting about registered sex offenders in the neighborhood, a taxation matter, or the possible loss of a school's accreditation. More recently, political candidates for national office have taken to holding town meetings or using a "town meeting" format to talk and listen, leaning on the lovely promise of the phrase, embedded in American local history. Town meetings are in *towns*—bounded communities where there are feelings of familiarity and shared destiny. An unspoken assumption of the town meeting is that if you take the time and trouble to come out, often on a weekday evening, then both the issue at stake and the persistence of the community matter immensely to you.

The use of the label "town meetings" for the health care discussions by legislators themselves, by the president, and by the media presented some baggage: These meetings, at their best, are assumed to be models of rational discourse, or at least some sort of meaningful, reciprocal exchange. This assumption was often overturned or rejected in the summer of 2009. Some cases were worrisome and some simply bizarre or comical. Most participants came to talk, listen, or both, but the nature of the health care reform debate brought out marginal and violent behaviors as well. There were those who arrived at their town meetings with posters of President Obama portrayed as Adolf Hitler, and others called him a socialist or communist. We witnessed many "take America back" themes, labeling Democratic proposals as dangerous. Pushing and shoving occurred at a variety of town meetings among those who held opposing views. And in some localities (in Arizona and New Hampshire, for example) the open display of guns and other weapons became a nonverbal form of protest against the president's reform ideas. (This practice, while not quite in keeping with the town hall meeting notion, was typically legal, and the Obama administration supported it in practice, if not in theory.)[18] But the most common form of negativity was disruption of the proceedings through yelling, shouting, and verbal assault, typically directed at the host legislator.

It is impossible to determine the percentage of town hall meetings that were disrupted by concerned, frightened, or in some cases, seemingly violent or mentally challenged individuals. But there is no question that the more disruptive town hall meetings (captured extensively on YouTube) tended to attract significant media attention, certainly across the Internet, but on the evening cable and network news broadcasts as well. One of the most frequently broadcast chaotic town meetings on health care was held by Representative Kathy Castor, a Democrat from the eleventh district of Florida. It bore little resemblance to the Norman Rockwell vision, with shouting, menacing bodies, and chanting.[19] The *St. Petersburg Times* reported:

"Tyranny! Tyranny! Tyranny!" dozens of people shouted as U.S. Rep. Kathy Castor, D-Tampa, struggled to talk about health insurance reforms under consideration in Washington, D.C.

"There is more consensus than there is disagreement when you get right down to it," Castor offered, immediately drowned out by groans and boos.

She pressed on, mostly unheard among screams from the audience estimated by Tampa police to be about 1,500. "Tell the truth! Tell the truth!" "Read the bill!" "Forty million illegals! Forty million illegals!"[20]

Health care reform was such a complex and emotionally fraught issue in the summer of 2009 that these town meetings might have been violent, disrupted, and unconstructive even if passionate expression had not been encouraged by anti-Obama (and generally anti–Democratic Party) forces. But there were organized, sustained efforts from the start, developed by Republican or Republican-allied groups and individuals, focused on controlling, or at least influencing, the nature of town hall meetings. In near perfect alignment with the themes of this book, the strategic use of incivility was pursued as a way to disrupt the meetings, garner media attention to the disruptions, and shape the national debate and the public policy outcomes themselves.

And there were effects, even if difficult to prove definitively. For example, at this writing, the negativity that surfaced at town hall meetings might well have caused a shift away from a "public option" for those Americans without health care coverage to a system of health care cooperatives. It is not possible to prove causality, but the Obama administration was forced to regroup in August, and they did back off at least some of their original proposals in the face of town meeting anger or more likely, widespread coverage of that opposition.[21] A leading Republican senator in the reform debate, Charles Grassley (Iowa), noted that the volatile, angry, town meetings convinced him that the reforms under discussion were too ambitious, and a scaled-back approach was needed.[22]

What were the "instructions" to citizens opposed to Obama's ideas? An early document, cited at the start of disruptive town hall meetings, was a memo titled "Rocking the Town Halls—Best Practices" by Bob MacGuffie, a political activist based in Connecticut.[23] The memo, published on the Web site Right Principles, contains a well-organized, extraordinarily clear, practical set of instructions on how to control and influence town meetings. MacGuffie suggests that an activist's "playbook" should lean on time-honored activist methods (he even cites left-wing activist Saul Alinsky of mid-twentieth-century Chicago) for gaining power in public settings: Be knowledgeable about the issues, know the legislator's record, prepare questions in advance, use quantitative evidence, meet beforehand to organize with others, bring protest signs, and develop press releases where possible. MacGuffie then becomes very specific in his advice, in a section about how to behave in the meeting:

> You need to rock-the-boat early in the Rep's presentation. . . . Don't carry on and make a scene—just short intermittent shout outs. The purpose is to make him uneasy early on and set the tone for the hall as clearly informal, and freewheeling. It will also embolden others who agree with us to call out and challenge with tough questions. The goal is to rattle him, get him off his prepared script and agenda.

He continues:

> When the formal Q & A session begins get all your hands up and keep them up—be persistent throughout the entire session. Keep body language neutral and look positive to improve chances of being selected. When called on, ask a specific prepared question that puts the onus on him [the legislator] to answer. It can be a long question including lots of statistics/facts. You will not be interrupted from reading a solid question. . . . The balance of the group should applaud

when the question is asked, further putting the Rep on the defensive. If the Rep tries a particularly odious diversion, someone from the group should yell out to answer the question. These tactics will clearly rattle the Rep and illustrate some degree of his ineptness to the balance of the audience.

The behavior at many of the more volatile town meetings reflected MacGuffie's advice (spread by other activists and reported by media), although he cannot claim credit for the disruptions at all meetings. The memo is striking for its hard-nosed, practical, traditional organizing emphases—the methods that have worked for the left and the right in American politics and far beyond. The strategic use of incivility is encouraged and elaborated, and MacGuffie even outlines what users of the method might expect if they are successful (e.g., local media coverage, persuasion of others, setting the legislator and staff "back on their heels," and so forth). The methods outlined in the memo may not be new—far from it, they are well practiced by many. But what is new is the ability to reach so many across the nation with these instructions, through Web posting and e-mail transmission. Just as national political campaigns try to get activists "on the same page" with regard to message and tactics, those who believe that the strategic use of incivility can work now have the very same options.

The memo, and the town hall meetings more generally, resonate with two other themes in this book: the unnerving nature of uncivil behavior (how it makes us feel) and our general need for interactivity and reaction, to what we think and feel. The town hall meeting and reactions to it on the Internet—watching meetings, blogging about them—fit well in our communication culture. In fact, the town hall meeting, designed for interaction and reciprocity, is writ large on Web sites, so we have the "in-person" town meetings at localities around the nation, then the ongoing Web conversations they inspire. A look at any of the raucous town meetings posted to the Web leads one to scores, sometimes hundreds, of comments about the meeting. Far from having a traditional structure and impact, the health care town hall meetings of 2009 were as modern as they could be: They were covered by conventional journalists and by amateurs, posted to the Web, discussed, debated, mocked, reedited, and so on. A single town meeting lives on in the American Web archive for years to come, able to impact those who attended and those who lived nowhere near it. Strange for a "town hall meeting" which was designed to promote discourse and action within a community of connected, empathetic neighbors.

The use of incivility was strategic, but also emotional in many cases. There was vehemence and either real or feigned anger and fear (fear of Obama's policies and even his personage as "socialist," for example). Some of the emotion, mostly anger, may have been fueled by media personalities, and many fingers point to Fox News. At the Tampa rally discussed earlier, for example, many attendees noted to the *Times* that they had been encouraged by Glenn Beck of Fox. Beck is a popular and emotional figure on Fox, and his Web site extends his ideas on politics. In this essay, Beck discusses the town meetings and, as in his television appearances, tries to give his conservative adherents the emotional strength to carry on:

> The great thing is you know that almost everybody in Washington has no spine. Find yours because I know you have one. Find yours. . . . Don't be intimidated. That's what they do. And don't you dare swing back because that's what they want you to do. That's what they need you to do. That I believe is what we're being set up for. They are already planting the seeds on it's the crazy tea partiers that just want to destroy the country and set it on fire. No, it's not. Don't play into it.[24]

Beck is compelling to many, but as we saw in Chapter 2, Sarah Palin is even more compelling. She is expert in the injection of emotion into debate and has a keen ability to give comfort to conservatives in the face of conflict. While no longer governor of Alaska, she was an active political voice in the summer of 2009. Using her Facebook page as a communication outlet, she wrote about Obama's health care proposals in early August.

> As more Americans delve into the disturbing details of the
> nationalized health care plan that the current administration
> is rushing through Congress, our collective jaw is dropping,
> and we're saying not just no, but hell no!
> The Democrats promise that a government health care
> system will reduce the cost of health care, but as the econ-
> omist Thomas Sowell has pointed out, government health
> care will not reduce the cost; it will simply refuse to pay the
> cost. And who will suffer the most when they ration care?
> The sick, the elderly, and the disabled, of course. The Amer-
> ica I know and love is not one in which my parents or my
> baby with Down Syndrome will have to stand in front of
> Obama's "death panel" so his bureaucrats can decide, based
> on a subjective judgment of their "level of productivity in so-
> ciety," whether they are worthy of health care. Such a system
> is downright evil.[25]

Palin's mischaracterization of voluntary palliative care counseling—hardly a new or even controversial aspect of medicine—took
hold. Word of "death panels" spread wildly through news channels
and the Web, forcing President Obama to respond at a town hall
meeting in New Hampshire: "The rumor that's been circulating a lot
lately is this idea that somehow the House of Representatives voted
for 'death panels' that will basically pull the plug on grandma because
we've decided that it's too expensive to let her live anymore."[26] It is
not clear why the President felt the need to respond to what was a
false, inflammatory claim, but he likely wanted to extinguish it early
in order to move on.

Palin, however, kept at it, adding this entry days later:

> Also this week, Alaskans will join Senators Murkowski and
> Begich in town hall meetings to discuss the current health
> care legislation. There are many disturbing details in the cur-
> rent bill that Washington is trying to rush through Congress,

but we must stick to a discussion of the issues and not get sidetracked by tactics that can be accused of leading to intimidation or harassment. Such tactics diminish our nation's civil discourse which we need now more than ever because the fine print in this outrageous health care proposal must be understood clearly and not get lost in conscientious voters' passion to want to make elected officials hear what we are saying. Let's not give the proponents of nationalized health care any reason to criticize us.[27]

Palin does not apologize for previous mischaracterizations of palliative care, but instead calls for civility. Interestingly, her call for civility is a strategic one. It argues: *Let us act civilly not because it is a democratic goal in itself, but because civility will enable us to be effective in fighting the "outrageous" proposal.* I emphasize this point because of what is missing: a more general warning to her supporters that opponents might have something valuable to say, or that dialogue—democratic *conversation*—might get us somewhere, productively.

Palin and Beck are a new breed of conservative media figures who seem to understand that others need to talk out loud just as they do. But neither seems to see the particular value of rational engagement that might come with talk—dialogic talk. Or at least they have been unable to articulate the value of debate in their more widespread public statements to date.

Not all the town meetings about health care in the summer of 2009 were raucous, violent, or even exciting. Many legislators held peaceful, productive ones, characterized by substantive exchanges and understanding. But attendance might have been lowered in some cases by the fear disrupters created or, in particular, fear of the spectacle the media showed on a nightly basis. A meeting of more than 1,000 people in Eugene, Oregon, was conducted with concern, dialogue, and peaceful exchange. One citizen, Herb Severson, was relieved by its civility: "I thought it was respectful. I was worried. I really was. I thought . . . based on the press and what you see on

TV there'd be people yelling and screaming and you'd see protests everywhere."[28]

Was it only Fox News and the Web—videos on YouTube, for example—that scared citizens like Mr. Severson? Or was there a more widespread fascination, on the part of other conventional media, with the chaotic, menacing, and violent town meetings? Media feed intensely on each other, and when it came to town meetings and civility, a massive number of clips showing rowdy behavior were captured by obscure outlets, then passed on to conventional media for broadcast. For example, many mainstream media, in addition to Web sites, played and replayed aggravated Massachusetts congressman Barney Frank's exchange with a young woman, holding up a picture of Obama portrayed as Adolf Hitler:

> While Frank attempted to respond to all questions, he gave up when one woman compared health care proposals favored by Frank and President Obama to policies of Nazi Germany.
>
> "When you ask me that question, I'm going to revert to my ethnic heritage and ask you a question: On what planet do you spend most of your time?" Frank asked. "You stand there with a picture of the president defaced to look like Hitler and compare the effort to increase health care to the Nazis," he said, adding such behavior demonstrated the strength of First Amendment guarantees of what he called "contemptible" free speech.
>
> "Trying to have a conversation with you would be like trying to argue with a dining room table," Frank said to the woman. "I have no interest in doing it."[29]

The Pew Research Center's Project for Excellence in Journalism (PEJ) followed the media coverage of health care in August, finding that it dominated the news (print, broadcast, and online) but was driven by cable networks. During a week in mid-August, the coverage was oriented primarily toward politics and protests (as opposed to policy or background journalism on health care problems). Numbers do not quite describe the texture of the town meetings, and in fact one could not understand the particularly odd dynamics of the town hall meeting by reliance on statistics alone. But they are helpful: "The 13 cable and radio talk shows studied by PEJ had an even more intense focus. Fully three quarters (75%) of the airtime studied in this talk universe was devoted to the health care issue last week. As the News Coverage Index has shown, talk shows tend to amplify the most polarizing political issues and last week, coverage of the hot-button topic seemed to literally boil over."[30]

Did the media take time, in their coverage or in replayed coverage from other outlets, to look to their own role in the rancor? Those strategic users of incivility prompted by activist MacGuffie aimed to pull media in, but how did mainstream media reflect upon their own activity?

As we saw in Chapter 2 when discussing the Palin campaign rallies, media stay away from comparative questions: What percentage of the health care town meetings were raucous, and how many were calm? Did particular areas of the nation produce more chaotic town meetings? Particular legislators? How often were activists linked to problematic town hall behavior, and how much was "organic"? Very few of these kinds of questions were asked or answered by media. They engaged in only the most cursory self-reflection, whether cable television news, conventional news, or popular Web sites (e.g., the Huffington Post). On rare occasions individual commentators alluded to deficiencies in media coverage. One of the few sustained looks at the media coverage of town halls came from Jon Stewart, the comedian who hosts *The Daily Show*.

Though journalists have been slow to critique themselves, Americans more generally are quite critical of the media. In fact, citizens judge the media to have done a stunningly poor job in covering the health care debate:

The latest News Interest Index survey, conducted July 31–August 3 among 1,013 adults by the Pew Research Center for the People and the Press, finds that the public gives news organizations low marks for their coverage of health care. More than seven-in-ten say the media has done either a poor (40%) or only fair (32%) job explaining details of the various proposals. Just 21% offer a positive rating of this coverage: 4% excellent and 17% good.

A similar percentage say news organizations have done either a poor (37%) or only fair (33%) job explaining the effect the "proposals would have on people like yourself."[31]

Apparently, while the raucous town meetings made for exciting television and YouTube content, the public did not find the talk at meetings particularly helpful in understanding the issues. There was certainly a way to cover civility and incivility while *also* educating viewers and readers. But as is often the case, media had trouble locating this more balanced form of public policy coverage.

It would be difficult to argue that strategic incivility was good for democracy in this case, although it was certainly a highly effective tool to disrupt the town meetings and shift the entire national debate. Obama was weakened by the vivid scenes of unhappiness—some of which did spring from the "grass roots" even if encouraged by well-organized political machines, and even if the town halls brought out a few marginal people of dubious mental health. In time, we will see the ultimate impact on Democratic policy proposals, but it is undeniable that the opposition broadened debate, used the interactive media tools now available, and sought comfort in their fellow activists. The three arguments I made about civility at the start of this book are helpful, and indeed omnipresent, in the 2009 health care town hall meetings.

Might Democrats—or at least those supporting Obama's policies—have been more thick-skinned about the Republican tactics at the town hall meetings? Would there have been a way to develop a resistance to incivility that might have saved the discourse in many meetings? Just as incivility is a strategic asset, a real skill when practiced well, listening and dealing with incivility can also be both skill and asset. Neither ignoring nor capitulating in the face of incivility will move a conversation. As we discuss in Chapter 5, these problems might better be solved by using a different structure for public debate. The contemporary town hall may evoke fond memories of a Rockwellian era, but it has no real structure. Is it any surprise that a few unhappy people, intent on disruption, can rule the day and dominate media? Do we encourage such negative, loose behaviors by having so little structure? Are town hall meetings set up for failure, given the lack of debating skills on the part of our citizenry? There are productive ways to conduct town hall meetings, but only when we first have built the culture of argument a modern democracy truly demands.

One last note on the town hall health care debates concerns the president. His Notre Dame speech called for civility; after the summer town halls he felt this need even more deeply. His statements during the health care debate mirrored those at Notre Dame, welcoming rigorous debate, urging calm, and asking people to talk "with" each other and not "over" each other. But unlike abortion, where people know how they feel and opinions are generally very stable, health care reform was a complex morass of plans, preferences, fears, data, and studies. There was much greater opportunity for misinformation, exemplified by the Palin "death panels." So Obama added a new dimension to his thoughts; misinformation can grease the wheels of incivility and needs to be confronted if civility is to be possible. He said in New Hampshire in the summer of 2009:

> That's what America's about, is we have a vigorous debate. That's why we have a democracy. . . . I do hope that we will talk with each other and not over each other. Because one of the objectives of democracy and debate is that we start refining our own views because maybe other people have different perspectives, things we didn't think of. Where we do disagree, let's disagree over things that are real—not these wild misrepresentations that bear no resemblance to anything that's actually been proposed.[32]

Growing civility in our times while dealing with the increasing amount of misinformation and poor data now available day or night across the Web presents another burden for someone often called Professor in Chief.

## Civility in the Obama Years

Many speeches, as well as conflicts like health care reform, await a new president, but the Notre Dame speech—in its grandeur and ambitions—gives us some sense of where the president might be headed with regard to his notions of both public opinion and civility. He is not naïve about the difficulty of finding common ground on difficult issues, seeing what he believes as the inherent failings of all people. But through his rhetorical techniques of frame shifting and redefinition of the problem, he tried to lay out another course on abortion at Notre Dame. One gets the sense that he could, as other presidents have done, apply his rhetorical weapons to other entrenched social issues as well, and perhaps we shall see this effort in the years to come.

My point is that civility and a deeply conflictual philosophy about public opinion will likely reappear as themes in Obama's rhetoric and approach to politics; he feels a great comfort level within these tensions. Whether or not this is a promising path is well beyond the scope of this book, and it is early in his presidency, but students of politics would do well to watch for the tendencies we see here. Will Obama—as a rule—turn to groups (interest groups, age groups, organizations) as his *solution* to difficult public policy debates as they appear, given that he does recognize entrenched, passionate, and organized interests as the problem? Will we see his administration value the study and navigation of interest group dynamics over what polls tell them? Does the focus on civility and respectful talk just keep us in respectful stalemate, or is it actually a tool for progress on tough issues? Finally, does a philosophy such as his—a largely pragmatic one—guide his own actions or is it reserved for high-minded public addresses?

Obama speaks directly to the themes of this book, seeing civility as a strategic asset more than as a state of the nation. As I argued in Chapter 1, civility is best viewed in this tactical light, because it is used so often in just this fashion. Societies are not inherently either civil or uncivil. Individuals and groups may act in one or the other of these ways, at different moments and for varying purposes. But to characterize any nation as becoming more or less civil is both empirically vacant and not particularly useful in political analysis. Sarah Palin uses civility (she is often warm, respectful, and humanitarian), but she employs incivility as well to energize her rally participants and engage her opponents. I do not mean to say that Obama is civil and Palin is not; both are politicians with a past and a future, and both will use the rhetorical techniques they need to pursue their goals, whether we admire those goals or not. But I urge analysts of political discourse and action to attend to how candidates and presidents *use* civility for their strategic purposes.

In a recent essay on Obama, writer Jonathan Chait argues that there is something called the Obama Method. He posits that the Method works in two steps, like this:

1. Find common ground and show respect for an opponent; declare hope for a resolution.
2. Note that the approach may or may not be effective, but trying is in itself an action of potentially great impact.

This is interesting to us, in that the approach inserts civility as a strategic weapon of the first order but simultaneously downplays it as a weapon. The ultimate effect may come from the expression of civility, but the target of the expression may not be the one you first or primarily focused on. Put another way, as Chait notes in the case of Middle East conflict: "Obama thinks he can move moderate Muslim opinion, pressure bad actors like Iran to negotiate, and, if Iran fails to comply, encourage other countries to isolate it. The strategy works whether or not Iran makes a reasonable agreement."[33]

During the 2008 presidential campaign, journalists and supporters sometimes compared Obama to Abraham Lincoln. Some noted that both eloquent leaders both hark from Illinois, while others were fascinated by the ironic, historical "full circle": an African American might hold Lincoln's office, when it was Lincoln who fought for the emancipation of slaves against strong opposition. Regardless of how the comparisons began, the Obama campaign was grateful for them and pursued events and symbolism to keep the ties to Lincoln strong, such as launching his campaign from Springfield and using it as the venue to introduce vice presidential candidate Joe Biden. Few deny Obama's capacity to move a crowd with his words, and Lincoln stands out as a president who valued language as well. But as the historian Sean Wilentz noted, in reviewing a spate of books published on Lincoln's two hundredth birthday, both the former president and Obama are poorly understood by literary critics and historians. He argues, from a position of deep respect for both leaders, that Lincoln—and now Obama—is in danger of tremendous distortion. Lincoln gave some great speeches, some real duds, and some that were not seen as great until long after his death. Most of all, Wilentz notes, he was a politician, something lost in the many attempts to paint Lincoln as a racist (the critique from the left) or a god who led America to a higher moral ground. Neither is the case, and Wilentz asks us to keep this fact in mind about Obama as well, regardless of the seemingly persuasive and nonpartisan nature of his speeches:

> Our president is hardly the innocent that he tries to appear to be, but it is precisely his intensely political character, the political cunning that lies behind all of his "transcendence" of politics, that makes him Lincolnian; and it comes as a great relief from the un-Lincolnian sanctimony that surrounds his image.[34]

Analysis of the Notre Dame speech, one explicitly bent on transcendence of politics, still needs to focus squarely on Obama the politician. This approach demeans neither the man nor the speech, but humanizes him as the partisan leader he is.

Whether or not presidential speech *matters* in persuading the public remains—after more than two hundred years—an open question. Wilentz argues that Lincoln's and Obama's speeches did.

While we should keep pursuing this "effects" issue with the best methodological tools and data, the unfortunate truth is that clear and quantifiable effects of presidential speech are slipping further and further from our grasp. It may seem simple enough to demonstrate some correlation of a speech and changes in public opinion, but this is far from the case, and one culprit is the Internet. Before the Web provided all presidential speeches as a de facto archive, and before amateur and professional comedians and ideologues began to edit the speeches for their purposes, a presidential speech stood out as a singular moment. A president gave a speech, journalists reported it, and people listened to it. Today a president's speech can live and impact an audience for years, shaping the public's ideas and values. But it can also get lost in the flood of media and authoritative voices it competes with. History, not the social science of the moment, will judge the effects of Obama's speech on civility, abortion discourse, and openness.

Let us not forget that Obama's speech was at a university commencement, his focus on young people graduating from college. He might have delivered an address on civility and abortion anywhere—certainly he received many invitations from groups either conflicted about or vehemently opposed to his views on abortion. But he chose this venue, a place that trains citizens, professionals, and future leaders. The next chapter is devoted to a major survey of American college students at a variety of public institutions—two-year colleges that focus on access for all, four-year universities, historically black institutions, commuter campuses, and elite research universities.

Obama spoke to all Americans in his address at Notre Dame, but it was devoted in large part to students. He urged them to seek common ground, to be lighthouses and crossroads. But do our college students have the sensibilities, the tools, or the real desire to follow their new president's instructions? As we will see, many young people do, but many others see political debate as worrisome and dangerous. Deeply embedded in the culture of campuses is a concern about tolerance and how to achieve it, given the diversity of opinion all around. Taking together Obama's speech and the real opinions of the students he aims to persuade, we find a far more complex picture of just how difficult civility is to attain in contemporary American political culture.

# 4 / Our Future Leaders

## *College Students and Political Argument*

President Barack Obama urged the 2009 graduates of Notre Dame to create a civil discourse for themselves and generations to come (see Appendix I). But are our students inclined in this direction, or capable of it?

As with nearly all social practices and norms, we learn our political manners and develop our ideas about civility early in life. The political socialization literature teaches us that young people pick up cues, ideals, party identifications, attitudes, and values from media, parents, teachers, coaches, ministers, and the other adults who populate their worlds. The importance of a young adult's environment has led political scientists, sociologists, psychologists, and others to study early family settings, churches, neighborhoods, and the educational experience from kindergarten through high school. The same researchers are often drawn to university settings as well, since they are the political socialization "worlds" where ideas are articulated most boldly by young people. Scholars have—since the earliest days of social science in the United States—scrutinized their students. They work closely with undergraduates and see them representing the future American citizenry and leadership, hence their chronic attraction to professional students of politics and cultural life.[1]

This chapter focuses on campus civility—how students talk with each other and the tensions associated with talk and argument. While I raise issues of "free speech" in passing, a topic in higher education over the past decades, I am less concerned here with rights than with the texture of actual practice: how political interactions make students feel, as well as the dialogic nature of the conversation. We introduce these themes as crucial to discussions of civility in Chapter 1, and the largely unregulated and informal nature of campus speech is an ideal place to explore civility.[2]

Here I focus on my home state of Georgia, a large southern state with significant urban, suburban, and rural populations. Expanding quickly, with immigrants from within and without the United States, Georgia is one of the ten fastest-growing states.[3] Often touted as an exemplar of the "New South," Georgia has tremendous diversity across race, class, and ethnicity. Agriculture is a dominant business, in addition to a variety of international corporate headquarters in multiple industries (e.g., transportation, communications, and manufacturing). Democrats largely controlled the Georgia statehouse and governor's office from the end of Reconstruction in 1876 until the beginning of the twenty-first century. At present, Republicans comfortably control both branches.

## Georgia's University Campuses

The state of Georgia has one of the largest systems of public higher education in the nation, and unlike many states, one system includes all types of academic institutions: It contains sixteen two-year colleges, fifteen four-year or "comprehensive" universities that grant some graduate degrees (three are historically black colleges), a medical and health sciences university, and three research universities (the University of Georgia, Georgia Institute of Technology, and Georgia State University). Taken together, enrollment at these institutions is just over 302,000, and the colleges and universities cover all regions of the state. An eighteen-member governor-appointed Board of Regents is responsible for the entire system, and, of course, all college and university presidents are also accountable to legislators and a variety of other stakeholders.

For several years and during multiple legislative sessions (each session in Georgia is two years in length), several representatives have been interested in "intellectual diversity." This concern is part of a national movement to ensure that colleges and universities protect free speech and prevent professorial bias in the classroom and beyond. Proponents of intellectual diversity have been particularly concerned about liberal and left-wing bias on college campuses throughout the nation. Whether their concerns are justified or not, in various regions or periods, is not the focus of this chapter. But legislative interest in the issues surrounding free speech and political talk motivated the research in this chapter, which I conducted in collaboration with general assembly members.

The proposed Georgia legislation on "intellectual diversity" is worth discussing, since it reflects a national movement, as well as data collections about student attitudes around the United States. The legislation has not been moved for a vote, and it can only suggest action to the Board of Regents. It is House Bill 154, introduced in 2007, the Intellectual Diversity in Higher Education Act. The central provisions, under Section 2, charge the Georgia Board of Regents to take the following steps, for each of the thirty-five campuses:

1. Conduct a study to assess the current state of intellectual diversity on its campus.
2. Incorporate intellectual diversity into institutional statements, grievance procedures, and activities on diversity.
3. Encourage a balanced variety of campus-wide panels and speakers and annually publish the names of panelists and speakers.

4. Establish clear campus policies that ensure that hecklers or threats of violence do not prevent speakers from speaking.
5. Include intellectual diversity concerns in the institution's guidelines on teaching and program development.
6. Include intellectual diversity issues in student course evaluations.
7. Develop hiring, tenure, and promotion policies that protect individuals against political viewpoint discrimination and track any reported grievances in that regard.
8. Establish clear campus policies to ensure freedom of the press for students and report any incidents of student newspaper thefts or destruction.
9. Establish clear campus policies to prohibit political bias in the distribution of student fee funds.
10. Eliminate any speech codes that restrict freedom of speech.
11. Create an institutional ombudsman on intellectual diversity.[4]

In the wake of discussion about this proposed legislation, we conducted surveys of all undergraduate students in the state over a two-year period (see Appendix II). The surveys revealed extraordinarily interesting findings with regard to political civility, putting aside the free speech matters that motivated the original study. Civility is, of course, our central concern here, although free speech is often related to—and sometimes even conflated with—civility.[5]

## Survey Goals and Methodology

The main goals of the survey were to explore issues of free speech on behalf of the legislature and to avoid the need for a legislative solution to perceived campus problems. I designed the survey, with the University of Georgia Survey Research Center's James Bason, during the spring of 2008 and again in the spring of 2009. We asked for and received feedback and approval on the survey from legislative stakeholders.[6]

The surveys used a Web-based form. A probability sample yielded 1,220 completed interviews in 2008, 2,918 in 2009. Larger universities provided larger samples, so the University of Georgia and a few other institutions contributed many respondents. While Georgia Tech has a significant population of students from outside the state, most students in the university system are residents of Georgia. And the population center of the state is Atlanta and surrounding suburbs, so many universities are located in this region and draw students from it.[7]

Seventy-one percent of the students in the sample were white, 16 percent were African American, 5 percent were Asian or Asian American, and 4 percent were Latino. Four percent considered themselves "multiracial." Political ideology was split nearly evenly between those identifying themselves as Republicans or Democrats: 34.4 percent were either strong, moderate, or weak Republicans, and 34.1 percent were Democrats of the strong, moderate, or weak persuasion. Twenty percent considered themselves independents.

I report primarily on the quantitative data from 2008 here, to match the campaign period (the primaries).[8] However, I draw on both surveys in the qualitative remarks that follow, and all data are publicly available.

## Feeling of Freedom: Political Discussion and Respect

As noted in Chapter 1, a feeling that one can express a view with some degree of comfort is critical to civility. We live in a world where emotions—how we feel—are typically central to personal and professional interaction. We probed students about the classroom environment and whether they felt free to discuss important public issues in class. This feeling is, of course, made possible by professor and fellow students alike, since a classroom climate is determined by multiple parties. We found that most students felt this freedom (nearly 70 percent) and very few felt stifled in such discussions (11 percent).

Faculty fared well in this survey, and while it is—depending upon how it is done—acceptable for professors to share their views with students insofar as that enhances class content, students feel instructors can go too far. In response to the statement "Professors in my classes have sometimes inappropriately presented their own political views in class," students (over 70 percent) largely disagreed.

Interestingly, of the students who claimed that professors had inappropriately presented their own views in class, a majority noted that a student did try to argue back (62 percent). This strikes me as courageous, given the general anxiety students tend to have about arguing with professors.

The qualitative comments help us flesh out some of the more worrisome dynamics in the classroom, whether these are inherent in the power differential or perceived professorial behavior (we only have the student viewpoint in this survey). While the results are a good reflection on faculty generally, unhappy students were vocal about the lack of freedom they felt and their attendant discomfort.

In answer to open-ended questions, students had a variety of complaints about faculty:

> The professor was talking about hurricane Katrina right after it occurred and was stating racist remarks about how white people were the only ones saved and that rich white people don't care about black people. I felt extremely offended and I felt that it was inappropriate. She then continued to show us the video clip of Kanye West saying on national TV that George Bush doesn't like black people. (Respondent 148)[9]

From another student:

> One prof. is very conservative. I am conservative also, but I have cringed at some of the comments he's made regarding Obama and Clinton. A couple of black females have seemed

offended about his comments about blacks in general and Clinton as [a] woman president. (Respondent 467)

Another notes:

This was a very liberal professor (Sociology) who had a tendency to make statements that were politically charged toward his way of thinking. There were older non-traditional students, along with several police officers attending the class who disagreed with some of the statements the instructor espoused. During a discussion after class, we all decided not to take the professor to task regarding his political beliefs. We felt that discretion was the better part of valor and kept our collective mouth shut rather than take a chance of getting a lower grade based on our beliefs. (Respondent 722)

Classrooms are unique forums, not always representative of campus talk, but useful in understanding larger dynamics at a university. The classroom is a place where students can *practice* argument and learn to be citizens under watchful eyes and with a strong norm for etiquette and respect. Students monitor themselves carefully, after well over a decade spent sitting in classrooms, where they learned to behave in class long before they arrived at college.

It is political discussion outside the classroom that more likely reflects the campus climate and culture with regard to civility. There is no authoritative figure in charge, and students themselves set the tone. We asked students about the respect—or lack of respect—they perceived among other students with regard to political opinion (Table 4.1). Most students gathered around the neutral point in the scale, for reasons I speculate on in the next section. But 21 percent felt a distinct lack of respect. For students who noted that other students were not respectful, we asked them to explain, then coded these open-ended answers. Most of the answers fell in a general "disrespect" category, as outlined in Table 4.2.

## TABLE 4.1  STUDENT RESPECT

"To what degree do you feel students at your institution are respectful of the political opinions of all students at your institution?"

| Response | N | Percentage of Students |
|---|---|---|
| Not very much | 76 | 6.9 |
| 2 | 152 | 13.8 |
| 3 | 350 | 31.7 |
| 4 | 338 | 30.6 |
| To a great degree | 187 | 16.9 |
| Total | 1,103 | 100 |

The open-ended queries, asking students to elaborate on the lack of respect, are helpful in clarifying their views on civility. A large number of students, within the categories of Table 4.2, were disturbed by what they viewed as rude or harsh behavior.

One form of uncivil behavior students noticed was tearing down of campaign posters or flyers. A student reported, "A few months ago I was at a [university Democratic Party] meeting and we found out that some of the [Hillary Clinton] posters that we had put up were being torn down by a McCain supporter" (1110).

Another saw destruction of Republican materials:

During the recent presidential campaign, several posters representing facts about the various candidates in a very objective and level way were posted around my dorm. Within a week, the republican candidates' posters had been graffitied with obscenities and persecution toward the soldiers in Iraq. Being fresh out of the military, I was appalled, especially that the posters were allowed to remain up, even with the graffiti.

## TABLE 4.2 REASONS FOR DISRESPECT

"Please explain why you feel students aren't respectful of the political beliefs of others at your institution."

| Reason | N | Percentage of Students |
|---|---|---|
| Anti-Democrat/liberal | 23 | 12.9 |
| Anti-Republican/Conservative | 18 | 10.1 |
| No respect for views different from own | 94 | 52.8 |
| Other students ignorant, apathetic, or young | 21 | 11.8 |
| Had to do with race | 5 | 2.8 |
| Had to do with religion | 4 | 2.2 |
| Other | 13 | 7.3 |
| Total | 178 | 100 |

I have also come under great persecution from my fellow students for serving in the armed forces. (781)

The tearing down or destruction of campaign materials was viewed as offensive, but students reported significant face-to-face confrontations and negativity. One student took the time to describe a campus rally, where yelling overwhelmed talk:

On a larger scale, there are demonstrations in the quad area. When there was an anti-abortion group there demonstrating, people from the pro-choice camp felt the need to be there, and they were holding signs that said, "Keep your religion out of my uterus." I'm not saying that they did not have the right to be there; I would fight for that right. I'm just saying that it doesn't seem very respectful to be yelling and carrying on with a sign like that when another person is trying to talk about his own ideas. (518)

Students were offended by rudeness, no matter the form, and it worried and depressed them. One student found that the rudeness had seeped into his or her e-mail box: "Because I have had encounters with students who have called me names and cursed me in e-mails as a result of speaking up, period. I have just blocked them from all communication in order to avoid another confrontation" (1011).

I was a bit surprised by the general level of intensity and frustration students felt across the ideological continuum. This is a typical comment about rudeness, and it is a bit startling in its passion, given that most faculty these days consider students to be apathetic and with few opinions, in comparison to decades past:[10]

I personally feel that it is every person's right to have and express any opinion they want in regards to any topic whatsoever. Some students, however, mock or criticize these opinions or beliefs because they find them contrary to their own. I am completely for students who disagree with other people's opinions and believe that it is as much their right to vocalize their disagreement of a person's opinion as it is to have an opinion in the first place. However, some students feel the need to express their disagreement in a rude or condescending manner. I'm all for people having beliefs. But I absolutely despise rudeness. By all means disagree, but do it with some respect. (1179)

Upon closer scrutiny, much of the talk about rude or harsh behavior, when it comes to political discussion, seems to revolve around a particular notion: Students accuse each other of arrogance and certainty, of thinking that they are always right. This perceived closed-mindedness runs through many of the examples and anecdotes from respondents.

Some students found others inordinately smug and impossible to converse with when any controversial issues arose. One noted, "[Disrespectful students] are mostly naive, jaded, and disrespectful sheep that grew up in the suburbs that stand for nothing (religious, political, etc. . . .). [T]hey see the world as they want to see it" (701). Another notes that disrespectful students "think that there is only one opinion that is correct and that is theirs. They want to believe what they believe and wrongfully accuse you of something when they know nothing about who you are at all" (278). And many of the students seemed to think it was simply too late for other students to learn open-mindedness: "[Students are disrespectful] . . . because they have been socialized throughout life to believe that their opinions are more right than others" (203). Contrary to the image of college being a place to "find oneself" and learn from others, a number of students saw the campus as just the opposite—a place where *already-formed* citizens clash, stay with like-minded others, or avoid politics altogether.

## Race, Party Identification, and Respect

Among the interesting findings are feelings about respectfulness held by African American students in contrast to white students (these are the predominant ethnicities in Georgia). Black students see more respectfulness on campus than white students by 10 percent. In open-ended queries, white anger was articulated more often than anger on the part of African American students. One student noted:

> At [university], if you are white, it is very often that you are treated as if your opinion does not matter. If the topic of race is being discussed, and you would like to say something about your own race (if you're white) you are either disregarded or

viewed as a racist. This is a very often occurrence at [university]. (234)

But there were plenty of students concerned about racism against African Americans and religious groups as well. One minority student wrote that other students—knowing he supported then-candidate Barack Obama—said Obama was too different to fit in a White House always occupied by whites (628).

With regard to party identification, the Republican and Democratic students perceived respectfulness at about the same levels: 50 percent of Republican students rated their campuses mostly respectful, and 48.2 percent of the Democrats felt the same. Independent students were far less happy with the respectfulness of other students, at 33 percent. No doubt in a primary season like 2008, followed by a general election with significant and highly partisan passions, independents felt somewhat left out of the discourse.

Plenty of students were unhappy with levels of civility and often tied these to party affiliation, accusing the opposing party members of poor behavior, or just finding partisanship generally disruptive to mutual respect, as in this case:

As a member of SGA [the student government association], I find it rare that any students will bring up any party affiliation or whether they are liberal or conservative. The ones, however, that do bring forth their party affiliations seem to be on a mission to destroy other people's beliefs. This is why, in my opinion, that I feel as though students are not respectful to my political opinions, nor the opinions of other students on campus. (361)

There is no question that the presidential campaign heightened students' awareness of parties and party affiliation. A large number of students tied their thoughts about incivility to comments about the candidates and the parties. Much of the talk was seen as demeaning:

"I [attend] a very conservative campus. If you aren't a Republican or view the world in an even slightly leftist view, you're considered UnAmerican" (252). Another wrote, "I have heard way too much backtalk about the 'crazies' on the 'other' side. There isn't a sense of open mindedness to see the other person's point of view" (732).

As interesting as these perspectives are, the most compelling finding from the open-ended queries is that students seem to lack the tools to argue in a cordial, respectful manner. They are aggravated by what I would label "seemingly inherent" barriers to civility and dialogue, and their comments reveal strong emotion and a deficit in reciprocal, conversational skills. One theme that appeared often is that students judged other students to be simply too old or too "set in their ways" to be open to argument or even civility. There were many references to parents or place of origin—the suburbs, the South, a conservative family, and other demographic descriptors. One student writes about the constraints one finds in a small-town college with students drawn from the local region:

My institution is located in a small town with little cultural diversity. I had transferred from a larger school and had previously felt much more comfortable. I see a lot of extreme conservatives who know little about the rest of the world, and thus refuse to respect any opinion other than their own. I suppose small town colleges are meant for small town minds. (162)

Another wrote:

It is my opinion that because [university] has so many non-traditional students who have not been a part of an intellectual environment in some years, they are not well acquainted with the courtesies due to other students in an academic environment. Younger, more conservative students who live at home, may not have been part of an academic setting long enough to learn ways in which to disagree with another student without becoming argumentative. (11)

This thoughtful student and many others view "argumentative" as pejorative, something to be avoided.

Some students feel that their fellow students are already "fully formed" and therefore immovable in their opinions. But other respondents believe their fellow students are not quite ready to be formed or to engage in citizenly dialogue: "Unfortunately, most students are 18–20 years old and thus tend to be very exuberant with their views. This same age range usually has not had a 'pay your own way job' or paid taxes. For these reasons, political discussions with your typical student tend to be tedious and one sided" (452). And then there are accusations of ignorance: Other students cannot argue in a civil fashion because they just do not know enough to enter into a dialogue: "The students do not understand the issues at hand. This is the cause of problems most of the time" (695).

We find much evidence in the students' remarks that feelings are vital to civility in politics. Many expressed fear of starting an argument. This (along with a good dose of apathy among some populations) is likely the reason that so many students did not comment on the respectfulness question, choosing the neutral category. They avoid argument altogether and so have no idea whether or not others are respectful. One student wrote, "Many students aren't willing to see things from a different point of view . . . there are many that are respectful, but often . . . if students disagree about political opinions it may start an argument" (460).

There was fear also about how an argument might turn out. One student wrote:

The number of times I've seen students almost become violent with another student over politics is a big factor in why I think many students either aren't respectful or just don't care. From personal experience, I've been verbally attacked quite a few times for my political stance, despite being sure to [choose] my words carefully so as to not cause offense. (1084)

Another student argued that diversity of people and views is frightening and might somehow spin out of control:

> Whenever there are several diverse groups of people in a certain place, respect generally decreases. While there are many people that are respectful of others and views, there are also many that criticize due to somebody having a different opinion than their own. At my institution, there are people from many different cultures, races and economic standings. . . . [Politics] is a very touchy subject for many, and a conversation between people of different political beliefs would more than likely turn in to a very heated and disrespectful debate. (935)

While student comments about civility and political argument were revealing, we also tried to probe their intellectual values. So we asked a battery of questions about their expectations and hopes from their course work and university experience. Two questions in particular resulted in some stunning results that shed more subtle light on the reports of incivility and fear above. First, 72 percent of students agreed that it was important for them to always feel comfortable in class. This seems a very high figure, particularly because another 19 percent chose the neutral midpoint, leaving only 7 percent believing comfort not to be an issue. This seems strong evidence for at least one factor underlying the student anxiety we find: Feeling comfortable and unthreatened intellectually is a value many students share.

On one hand, this value placed on comfort is a good thing because it can be a challenge to teach and learn in an uncomfortable environment. But as faculty across many disciplines know, some discomfort can be extraordinarily helpful. Many times, challenges and arguments are critical to student development as citizens and intellectuals. The classroom, many scholars argue, is inherently safe, since it typically exists within a highly regulated campus environment. This fundamental safety then enables the classroom to be a place of real challenge and argument. What better place than the safe classroom to "practice" for a life of citizenship? It prepares students for the arguments that parents, employees, and community members face in the workplace, the PTA, boards, and other arenas of local democracy.

Students seek comfort in the classroom beyond the already-existing inherent safety a university setting generally offers. Faculty and students thus likely see the classroom a bit differently; where students desire comfort and even peace, their instructors at times prefer a somewhat more contentious atmosphere. Still, faculty need to heed student culture and expectations as they find them. After all, faculty are judged in part by student evaluations of their teaching, so in most cases instructors try to cope with attitudes about the classroom environment in ways that are not disruptive to their own careers.

It could be that students want comfort in the classroom in part because they simply do not know most of the other students. Students do, now and then, depending on the size of a university or department, share classes with close personal friends. But in most cases, their friends are elsewhere, and the fellow students in their courses are essentially strangers. When we asked students about the importance of debate with their friends, in contrast to the classroom, they were enthusiastic about argument. Nearly 65 percent of students believed it was important to them to debate with their friends, with 24 percent neutral and only 11.6 percent feeling that this was unimportant. These data give us a more textured sense of the issues: The classroom is worrisome, a place of strangers. The campus at large— the random interactions, e-mail, meeting behavior, poster destruction—also worries students, as we found in the open-ended queries. It is with friends that our students find the comfort to argue.

One might suggest that debate and comfort issues change by age cohort—that older students and upperclassmen are less concerned with these matters than younger students. Yet no significant differences were found across age cohorts. The same was true for race: African American and white students shared similar beliefs about these matters.

## A Note about Religion

The survey of students focused on politics and public issues, but for the sake of comparison, and because religion receives more attention in the American South than in some other regions, we also asked students about religious discussion on campus. Students were more likely to express opinions about politics than religion: 70 percent of students reported feeling free to discuss public affairs compared to 58 percent when it came to opinions about religion.

We asked students about their religious preferences. Fifty-seven percent of respondents claimed to be Protestant, 14.4 percent Catholic, 1.4 percent Jewish, 1.2 percent Hindu, 1 percent Buddhist, and 0.8 percent Muslim. Fifteen percent had no religious preference, and the rest said Other (9.4 percent).

The answers to open-ended queries about discomfort and incivility with regard to religious expression closely resembled those cited for politics: Other students are seen as ignorant, immature, closed-minded, and sheltered. Here we see differences in two students' perspectives and how campuses can vary in a diverse state like Georgia:

In the library there are slurs referring to Muslims and Allah carved into the wall in the silent study section. I realize that I am in a predominantly Christian area, but I feel that there could be more clubs that encourage tolerance for atheists, and other non-Christians. . . . Last semester . . . [when I told another student my major was anthropology] she actually said eww. (793)

The majority of the students here are neither Christian nor Jewish, and they feel that it is OK to make fun of both of these religions. There is a great deal of anti-Semitism here, but it is ignored by almost everybody. If you say one derogatory thing about Muhammad, then people will jump down your throat. Apparently it's fine though to use degrading comments about Jews. Also, if you claim to be a Christian, then you are almost as poorly received as if you were Jewish. It is also fine to offend Christians both behind their back and to their face. (87)

Although respondents were given as much room to discuss religious incivility as they were given for responses about political incivility, there was much less commentary. It could be that, despite some compelling examples of incivility from these two students, religion is seen as an acceptable area of real and tolerable difference among students. It is also possible that while students claimed religious affiliations, these are not held with particular intensity or passion.

## Civility and Strategy

One wonders how much students care about civility. They tell us it matters, and data from the 2009 survey validate this assertion, as noted in Table 4.3. When reading through the hundreds of student comments from the 2008 and 2009 surveys, it is clear that civility and incivility matter to students. There is an abundance of fear and passion about civility, as well as some real appreciation expressed by students who are happy with the tone of their campus.

Students—in their earliest days as voters and citizens—already see the possibilities for using civility and incivility as strategic assets. They do not accept good or bad behavior on its face, and even though they were not asked directly about strategic matters, they ended up writing about the "asset" that civility can be.[11] For example, one student notes tactics directly in 2009:

The only incivility on campus is those organizations that use shock tactics to entice interest. This includes the "God Hates

TABLE 4.3 IMPORTANCE OF CIVILITY

"How important do you think civility, that is, tolerance and respect for others' opinions, is to students on your campus?" (2009 survey only)

| Importance Level | N | Percentage of Students |
|---|---|---|
| Not at all important | 38 | 1.5 |
| Not very important | 152 | 6.0 |
| Average importance | 605 | 23.9 |
| Somewhat important | 556 | 22.0 |
| Very important | 1,179 | 46.6 |
| Total | 2,530 | 100 |

Fags" group as well as the Anti-abortion groups that use giant pictures of mutilated babies in public areas on campus. I am tolerant of these peoples' viewpoints, but I don't care to be yelled at or shown pictures of gore in the morning, regardless of how "true" they claim it to be. (474)

Another argues that students see through incivility, as a tactic: "Almost everybody is annoyed by those people [a group of local Christian activists], so nobody defends them, and most people laugh them off" (829).

We see that because students fear strong emotions or discomfort, they worry about starting arguments or finding themselves in a heated discussion. Comments about these anxieties are common, whether we asked students about the classroom or the campus as a whole. Students certainly feel more at ease with their friends, but there was little commentary about the *positive* aspects of political debate and discussion. As is so often the case, one of the most interesting aspects of the study is what's missing. In this instance, it is the absence of joyful talk about political interaction on campus: Few students spoke to the pleasures of political debate or the gratification one can feel in the heat or aftermath of a good argument.

I posit that fear of communication in this case is largely a cultural issue more than an individualized, psychological phenomenon, although, of course, personality matters. There is a fine literature on what scholars call communication apprehension, a fear of social interaction and public speaking in particular contexts. While this is an important notion, it does not help us much when it comes to civility, a largely sociological and political concept. There is no question that certain students are more anxious and fearful than others as a result of individual characteristics or tendencies. But the overwhelming evidence, from the intensity of students' comments, is that politics is broadly seen as a worrisome area to be avoided. Or if not avoided, political discussion and its messy, often uncontrollable aspects is something to be braced for and managed carefully in order to avoid social disaster.[12]

## Codes for Speech and Civility

While the surveys across scores of diverse institutions in Georgia are unique, campus administrators across the United States struggle with matters of civility. Presidents, vice presidents, deans, faculty, and others have grave responsibility for students, and the campus tends to be a closely watched microcosm of America. Campus activity—political, social, and cultural—has been a focus of American interest for a long while, although there was a tremendous surge in attention during the 1960s and 1970s because of the antiwar movement and racial strife. Journalists, statesmen, and citizens look to college campuses for cues about culture and the future. They are "minisocieties," and even social experiments, with large numbers of people living in close quarters around a singular institution. As a result of this attention, university faculty and administrators have given the matter of civility significant thought. The level of sophistication on some campuses is quite high, although primarily among faculty and administrators, either because of particularly difficult incidents that a campus survived or thanks to the leadership of a particular president or vice president.

The typical campus approaches to civility have been rule based and have treated civility as a strategic asset, one they care deeply about protecting and encouraging. Yet incivility as an asset is recognized in codes and rules as well, so it has its place, if a more worrisome one in the eyes of administrators. (Some campuses cordon off certain areas as "free speech zones" or "demonstration areas." One wonders: Are those zones for the practice of incivility only, while civility owns a bigger chunk of campus?) And in the case of campus administration, assets are protected by dictate. Rules tend to be the central framework for the pursuit of civility and avoidance of behavioral problems on campus. Like most arenas of American life, campuses are places where lawsuits and threats of suits abound, so attorneys have played a leading role in helping to review, construct, and apply regulations in order to avoid damages and danger to students and faculty.

A brief look at one set of campus rules, often called codes of conduct, is helpful and is representative of many campus efforts throughout the United States. From the document "Campus Civility and the Disruption of Learning: A Guide for Faculty and Staff," created by California State University in Long Beach, we get a sense of the ways in which many universities cope with what they see as the dangers of incivility. The guide gives examples of disruptive behavior—using obscene language, interrupting others, becoming belligerent, and so on—and instruction on how to deal with these behaviors, from the mild offense to true emergencies. It opens with this straightforward if legalistic paragraph:

> California State University, Long Beach takes seriously its tradition of maintaining civility and mutual respect among all members of the University community. These qualities are intrinsic to excellence in teaching and learning. They also

122 / Chapter 4

contribute to the maintenance of a productive workplace and an overall positive campus climate. . . . Nevertheless it is possible that faculty or staff may experience behavior that is disruptive to the learning/workplace environment or even personally threatening. These disruptions may happen in a classroom, department, faculty or staff offices, or others areas on the campus. Disruptions might be caused by members of the campus community, but may also be caused by people who visit the campus or by children of students or personnel. **Civility is the responsibility of everyone who participates on the CSULB campus** [*sic*]. Student behavior is governed by University policies, including the CSULB Student Code of Conduct. However, in cases in which a student has caused a disruption to educational or administrative activities, faculty or staff members may need to address issues related to the perceived safety to themselves and other members of the community. These guidelines were developed to provide faculty and staff with a range of responses to disruptive behavior.

The document lists resources for help, including contact numbers for the university ombudsman, the dean of students, the university police, the campus counseling services, and other offices. In the context of these documents more broadly, it is a well-organized, practical, and appropriate set of guidelines for the university community.[13]

Codes like this are a relatively new phenomenon, proliferating in the 1990s in response to changing views of college campuses by leaders, as well as some high-profile incidents involving hate speech around the nation. As Gerald Uelmen noted, "There were approximately 75 hate speech codes in place at U.S. colleges and universities in 1990; by 1991, the number grew to over 300."[14] No definitive count is possible, given the large number of institutions in the United States and the complexities of the codes: Many universities now have a series of behavioral codes, handbooks, orientations, "compacts" with students, and other mechanisms to control speech. The codes change and evolve, but they are a constant across type of institutions and seem to hold an authoritative place in university Web sites and materials. (They can, of course, also serve as a locus for fierce debates over "political correctness," an interesting topic not addressed in this book.)

What I find interesting about this fairly new breed of campus codes and guidelines is that they pair civility so closely with potential danger. "Civility" is linked with "disruptive behavior" in the title of the California State document, underscoring student responsibilities and the potential for problematic activities. Civility and its protection, in this guide as in many others, ends up with a list of rules, regulations, and campus offices.

It is a perfectly reasonable approach: Campuses, with so many young people and possibilities for harm, are places that need rules and resources made clear to students and staff alike, even beyond legal necessity. But the conundrum of civility remains: We, as citizens, live on campus for only a short while, if we are so fortunate as to be able to afford that luxury in these times. There are laws in life after college, of course, but no set of shared rules or norms set down on paper as clearly as one finds on today's campuses. And, most difficult of all for citizens, there is no truly authoritative figure to help us with balance: Where does contentious, passionate argument stop and incivility begin? It depends, of course, on the players and the context, and in my final chapter, I attempt to draw some lines, at least, and reflect on how to move forward in a new political century.

# 5 / Conclusion

## Civility, Communication, and
## a Culture of Argument

I would hope that everyone would go back to their
gentlemanly ways. . . . And I hope everyone will, as
I've said to a number of people, [recall] Rodney King:
"Let's just all try to get along."
> SENATOR HARRY REID during the congressional
> health care debate, December 22, 2009

A t the start of this book, I argued that civility and incivility
were strategic assets used by those pursuing specific interests,
whether humanitarian efforts or far less admirable ones. Civility
and incivility both have much to do with emotional comfort as well
as dialogue, hence their strategic use. These theoretical notions were
helpful in evaluating contemporary American politics: Sarah Palin
impressively used civility and incivility to move her rally crowds.
And President Barack Obama argued powerfully for civility in public
debate of abortion rights, our most contested social issue for decades.
Our themes turn up in dramatic fashion among university students,
more fearful of what such dialogue might bring than proud of their
newfound ideologies.

In an era where bipartisanship is both absent and seemingly
downright elusive on a national level, and where fringe elements
threaten our elected representatives with violence, civility might seem
an outdated concept, no matter how we try to approach it.[1] But we

should not allow the theatrical nastiness in Washington to prevent us from considering the deeper nature of American political culture and its possibilities. Partisanship and cooperation will come and go in the halls of Congress, and depending on the issues, sometimes on very short cycles. What is important is to sharpen our long-term focus on argument and how it might evolve in a civil society.

Getting to closure on the nature and uses of civility and incivility is complicated, and the complexity of the task is not surprising, given the long-standing debates about the topic. But by evaluating contemporary media, Internet discourse, the words of our political leaders, and the feelings of young people, we can see that the conversation about civility needs to change. We must recognize its shifting, often slippery meaning across periods, as many historians have already done, and be cognizant of precisely how civility is "practiced" in various media. When, on a typical day, we engage in conversation, read the newspaper, scan the Internet, or sit down for a few hours of television, we encounter a web of diverse manifestations of civility—from mean talk on blogs to the relatively civil Sunday talk programs on news networks. What do we pay attention to most, and which of these guides our behavior?

Many scholars and advertisers try to rank the import of each medium to American citizens. Yet there is no answer to the question of how we get our information, cues, and values. This is a frightful prospect for social scientists, but one that citizens increasingly accept. Many media "rent our eyeballs," often for hours, more often for seconds or minutes. Our menu of incoming and outgoing communications, whether from a keyboard or in person, illustrates the notion of "flow," put forth by the literary critic Raymond Williams decades ago. At a time when television dominated our media consumption, he argued that we must abandon study of particular texts or programs and try to study a full day or night of television—how the hours look to the analyst when taken together. But these days we determine our own idiosyncratic media menu through the choices we make, what we record, and how much attention we pay at any given moment. This can be terribly frustrating for the scholar trying to track how we keep up with the options for cognitive engagement forever flashing all around.[2]

Civility and incivility take too many forms to record in an era of such great fluidity of information and imagery. Despite the communicative chaos, fundamental tenets of democracy still guide scholars, elected officials, and American citizens. Civil discourse has long been a goal for advocates of democracy in emerging democratic countries, from the former Soviet states to Africa. But when our communications are so varied, so immediate, and so intense, how can we pursue and attain civility? Can and should we learn to champion and teach it, and to put uses of incivility in context, even when they unnerve us? As we saw with the Palin rally coverage, even our most prominent journalists have little context and few tools for understanding or placing passionate discourse.

This absence of sophistication is rooted in the lack of simple cultural "tool kits" for enhancing civility. The key both to the pursuit of civility and the tolerance of incivility where we find it lies in the creation of a *culture of argument* and debate, through nuts-and-bolts techniques well known to many educators. It is through argument and critique that students and adults learn best. And it is through argument that citizens can most fruitfully interact to strengthen local democracy and national political discourse. In addition to making argumentation central to education during vital years when young people learn to be citizens (middle school and high school), we need to learn skills of "hard listening"—making the best possible effort to *process* what is said to us. We can teach citizens to excel in basic argumentation, but at the same time we need a national approach to thoughtful listening as well, an idea that originated with political scientist Benjamin Barber. Both these paths can be pursued in person and through the Internet, and neither is a luxury. Without the development of a culture of argument and listening, instances of civility and incivility will be misunderstood, and both will be underutilized as strategic assets in building democracy.

## Comfort, Rules, and Debate

Many citizens fear passionate argument, worrying that it may lead to discomfort or even violence. We have seen this response in a fear of Sarah Palin's crowd behaviors among journalists and bloggers, in President Obama's deep concern with our inability to discuss contested matters, and in frightened attempts at political talk on the part of college students. The desire to avoid serious conflict, to "feel good" during political talk, has likely been heightened by the therapeutic and self-disclosing nature of contemporary culture. In the current climate, the proliferation of psychological helpers and self-help books encourages us to root out what makes us uncomfortable and unhappy, then work to eliminate these black spots on our psyches. If we regard civility and incivility as strategic assets that people use for good and ill, moments of incivility may be somewhat easier to withstand without significantly damaging ourselves. Put another way, we can evaluate political discourse that makes us feel bad, rooting it out for discussion, in the same ways we do our other problematic feelings.

One approach to these broad, mediated social issues is to look first to the study of bounded organizations. In this book, I have explored the nature of civility in the public sphere writ large—how citizens, journalists, candidates, and others act toward each other. But there are multiple studies of civil and uncivil behavior within corporations, organizations, schools, churches, and families. Organizations have different dynamics than the realm of mass communication, where words fly and there is so little accountability for one's expression of opinion. But we can learn from the best studies of civility in politics. One of these was the project conducted by Kathleen Hall Jamieson for the Annenberg Public Policy Center several years ago.

Jamieson studied pejorative speech forms used in U.S. congressional debate—insults, name-calling, hyperbole—and requests to have offensive words or phrases withdrawn from the official record. Among her findings are that concerted attention to civility—bipartisan congressional retreats centering on the topic, for example—

did have a clear positive effect on the respectfulness of discourse in Congress.[3]

Jamieson makes the point that her research on civility in Congress assumes that strong partisanship is not the driver of incivility: People can be passionate and civil at the same time (the very tension our college students in Chapter 4 struggled with). In addition to emphasizing the success of retreats, awareness of civility as a problem, and the measurement of uncivil behavior, Jamieson articulated multiple recommendations for members of Congress, actions that might produce the sort of productive discussion worthy of that body. She suggests a variety of approaches born of generalized proper etiquette (e.g., members should accept apologies if they are offered). And she also offers a series of more technical suggestions appropriate for Congress, given its rules of operation, such as establishing penalties for threats of violence, in addition to the existing penalties for unparliamentary speech.

While the bounded, highly regulated nature of a body like Congress presents less complexity than the control of civility in the overall public sphere, Jamieson underscores the importance of procedures—establishing them, making them clear, enforcing them. She suggests that political party members support each other but also police each other to some extent. Parties should choose skilled members to monitor their colleagues: "These individuals would be tasked with calming the Member and his/her speech before it oversteps the line, securing recognition to urge a change in the tone of debate."[4] This policing/monitoring notion is one that can be brought into the public sphere more generally. Even outside a rule-laden organization like Congress, there are ways that people can police each other and adhere to conventions. This is what social norms achieve—the idea that we will behave well if we fear isolation for misbehavior (as in John Locke's "law of opinion" described in Chapter 2).[5]

Jamieson's perception that civility has enjoyed some progress in Congress is not shared by everyone, especially when they see the uncivil congressional speeches highlighted by news media, by citizens posting events to YouTube, and by comedians. Among the most popular comics using congressional discourse as evidence of governmental and indeed societal incivility is Jon Stewart, host of *The Daily Show*, a nightly spoof of national news and events. He commonly shows hilariously uncivil moments from the floor of the House or Senate—members berating either each other or the witnesses they have summoned to testify. This is another layered phenomenon where incivility is used as a strategic asset: Members use it against each other or witnesses, for their purposes. Then Stewart grabs it for his metalevel comic purpose, a strategic tool to make us laugh at figures who we had hoped might behave in a more dignified manner appropriate to their positions.

Putting aside the comic strategies, incivility has been used to great effect on political talk shows. Sometimes these are set up as simple pro/con discussions, such as the highly restrained "Weekly Political Wrap" featuring Mark Shields and David Brooks on the *PBS NewsHour* with Jim Lehrer.[6] There are also larger panels on CNN, *Meet the Press*, and other well-known American channels and programs. Participants range from the calm and collected to the highly excitable, and the livelier and more conflictual the discussion, the more engaging it is according to many scholars.[7] Uncivil exchanges, while they are often quickly tamped down by a moderator or host, are expected by the audience and indeed hoped for: The best programs have worked strategic incivility into the format to make it interesting for viewers.

These forums are popular enough to have become a staple on many networks, but one does wonder about their long-term place in political talk. My prediction is that they will remain on the scene for a while, but that within a decade they may be largely replaced by Internet options offering viewers direct participation. At present, a limited number of citizens can call in to television or radio debate programs, but the options are slender relative to what might be possible through the Internet. As the technology for face-to-face communication and teleconferencing from one's own laptop improves and diffuses, and as Wi-Fi networks expand, citizens will increasingly form their own versions of political talk programs and chats. We shall see how these develop, how a new culture of "rules" is established, and how they affect larger political discourse.

My point is that incivility at times provides wonderful entertainment, but it creates anxiety. Congressional leaders have worried about civility enough to try to define it, sustain an awareness of it, and try to control it, through rules changes and even congressional retreats. While the public sphere well beyond Capitol Hill is vast and complex, we do see attempts at developing norms of civility on the Internet, as the net increasingly becomes the place to engage in political discussion among citizens and leaders. There are inchoate, if often clunky, attempts at monitoring speech, making rules, and teaching civility.[8]

## Revisiting Civility and Etiquette: The Internet

Although the Internet has profoundly changed the international communication environment, there have been fewer compelling scholarly studies of its effects than one might expect. This lack is primarily due to the nature of social science research: Careful study design and the collection of accurate data take time and money. As a result, we have seen a dearth of conclusive scholarly works, but a plethora of popular books on the effects of the Web on politics. Some are thoughtful and produce hypotheses that can be tested by researchers over time. Others are wildly speculative, assume effects that simply cannot be proven, and make claims that we cannot investigate using the methodologies of contemporary social science.[9]

Among the social scientific studies of political civility on the Web is Zizi Papacharissi's work on the nature of online discussion groups.[10] She evaluated 287 discussion "threads" in Usenet newsgroups that focused on politics. Newsgroups are places where people can post their views and comments when they like, as opposed to chat rooms where people are in direct, real-time dialogue. (Papacharissi notes that analyzing newsgroups is preferable, since the discussions tend to be longer and more oriented around issues than chat rooms.) Papacharissi found that incivility did not dominate the discussions, contrary to what one might expect, given the anonymity possible on the Web. Interestingly, respondents police themselves, as one sometimes sees on political Web sites:

> Most discussion maintained a calm and mild tone. Frequently, threads began with a call for action, a complaint about a policy, or a reference to a popular public debate. Usually respondents chatted about the issues at hand, until the discussion somehow escalated into a debate. This happened mainly when an opinionated participant expressed his/her take on an issue in an uncivil and/or impolite manner, or when a person put forth a fairly unusual and provocative point of view. The next five or six messages that followed would contain heated discussion, with occurrences of impoliteness or incivility. Eventually they would be toned down by the discussants themselves, who realized that their exchanges were reaching the point of nonsensical rants.[11]

The study also makes distinctions between what is uncivil and what is simply impolite (name-calling and cursing are impolite; sarcasm may just be a bit uncivil). But in general people were "calm and mild" in tone. Finally, and critical to our purposes here, Papacharissi emphasizes that civility and incivility are behaviors or rhetorical styles online. Again, these are strategic assets, not "end states," and her analysis of how these assets are used is highly productive as a result: By treating civility as a strategic weapon, we can trace Web discussion—how participants enter a conversation, how they swerve to debate or accommodate others, and often, how and why they apologize. Although previous chapters did not evaluate strings of Web conversation, my analysis of newsgroups, blogs, responses to blogs, and other apertures for Internet communication shows this area to be ripe for even more rigorous scrutiny.

In the continuing battles over free speech and media, some have made attempts to regulate civility on the Internet, failing to see the sort of self-regulation that Papacharissi found traces of in her work. One instance of attempted regulation arose in the New Jersey state legislature in 2006, when Assemblyman Peter Biondi introduced legislation requiring participants to use their names and addresses on local discussion boards. On the site in question, nj.com, name-calling and incivility were—according to the legislator—out of hand and needed to be curbed. As he told the *New York Times*, "Geez, . . . What happened to civility?"[12] The bill was unlikely to withstand legal review and was withdrawn (after Biondi's office was flooded with negative mail). But his point is one that has been made repeatedly in recent years, in much the same way that obscenity in television and movies has held a permanent place in the dialogue about media and free speech.

Journalists, bloggers, and others who watch the Internet and evolving sites seem to note a trend toward civility, despite the worries of legislators and assorted other public figures. Even the etiquette guru Miss Manners (Judith Martin) expresses optimism:

> If you recall, when the Internet first became wildly popular, it was supposed to be an etiquette-free zone. . . . But if you're saying, "You're stupid," sounding off and insulting each other, nothing of any substance gets said. What happened on the Internet was that people rediscovered an old truth about community life, which is that if you do not have some rules, nothing gets done. So gradually rules developed.[13]

There are other signs of concern about civility. We have all seen plenty of incivility on the Web, and we wonder whether heinous crimes committed over the Internet—fraud, stalking, and abuse leading to suicide—are somehow the extreme version of incivility. Perhaps it is fear, but much of it may be weariness with flaming that is more offensive than dangerous. Given this day-to-day aggravation, and our constant search for new communication forms, civility might just make a comeback.[14]

One thing is clear with regard to the Internet and television: Incivility is conflated with the fierce partisanship of American politics in 2010 as well as the attractions of uncivil behavior for making a profit. Journalists and editors—whether they work for a television network or run an Internet site—know that incivility is just more *interesting*, and therefore profitable, than civility. In a society where we seek the novel, media must try harder than ever to provide it to us. Contra McLuhan, the electronic media are not "cool" at all: Conflict sells and excites in ways that calm political dialogue never will. Scholars need to recognize this seemingly fundamental attraction we have to a good fight, or we will be ignoring both human tendencies and the need a profit-driven media has to play to them.[15]

How do we reconcile our weariness with incivility and our chronic attraction to it? There are no simple answers, of course, but thinking of civility and incivility as strategic tools does help a bit. Tools or technologies are things we pick up and put down, depending on context. If we can see them used this way, our disgust with incivility is lessened somewhat. By contrast, if we see incivility as a state of a society, it is difficult to break free from it—or to take some pleasure in it when it is in fact short-lived, benign, ridiculous, or entertaining.

Whether or not new norms of civility develop for the Internet, or only parts of the Internet, there are some marked improvements we can make as educators, statesmen, and journalists. Putting aside regulation, a notion that runs counter to the beauty and promise of the Web as a democratizing force, the goal should be to influence political culture at large—the way citizens think of each other, their communities, and democracy itself. If we work on these aspects of American political behavior, civility and incivility will be influenced greatly, whether on the Internet, on television, in magazines, in town meetings, in Congress, or in interpersonal discussion—indeed, in all places where political dialogue occurs.

## Influencing the Future of Civility: Debate

As we have seen, Americans—whether candidates, journalists, or young college students on campuses—are not sure how to handle debate. In particular, passion and argument coincide uncomfortably in our culture. One old bromide warns, "Avoid politics and religion!" at social events or in "mixed company." This underlying fear that argument could career out of control showed up everywhere in my study of students. Young people do not know where to draw lines or whether one can be passionate—even wildly so—and still maintain the sort of civility we hope to enjoy in day-to-day community life. We do have some excellent models of civilized, passionate debate— the more serious forums of pundits on Sunday-morning television or the highly regulated presidential debates. But these events are few and far between, and one might argue that they are civil but blood- less. The presidential debates are, in fact, a fine example of just how uncomfortable we are with passion in debate and how hard it is to blend civility, passion, and substance into argument.[16]

Presidential debates are the highest-profile debates we have in the United States, and they enjoy extraordinarily high viewership. Nielsen estimated, for example, that the first 2008 presidential debate between Barack Obama and John McCain was viewed by 57 mil- lion Americans (the record is the October 28, 1980, debate between Carter and Reagan, with 81 million viewers).[17] Activists, journalists, scholars, and citizens all critique problematic debate formats, uneven moderation, candidate attitude, constraints of setting, and other at- tendant challenges. There is likely no perfect format for these events, but the most consistent criticisms are that the debates touch on issues only superficially, that moderator follow-up is poor, and that con- versation between candidates tends to become unfocused and some- times impolite.

The problems in presidential debates resonate with the wider struggle over civility. Candidates tend to have great difficulty com- bining zeal and substance, and moderators tend to get nervous if passion rises. Fervor and enthusiasm take time to gain steam, but time limits and other format rules seem designed precisely to squash both. Moderators can refer to time constraints and switch to new subjects as a way to avoid what they see as rising incivility.

The bottom line is that our presidential debates do not provide a model for civil, passionate public discourse. So what is the model for us, one that might be learned in middle and high schools, applied on our campuses and in our communities, and then brought to the varied spaces of the Internet? Are there formats for debate and civil exchange that enable passion, civility, and substance? How can we begin to create a civilized "culture of argument" to carry with us, no matter the communication venue?[18]

There are a variety of ways for agents—teachers, journalists, bloggers, and leaders—to influence how Americans make arguments and structure debate, in person and online. Philosopher Stephen Toulmin laid out the characteristics of persuasive argument.[19] They are

1. **Claim:** the argument one would like believed by an audience.
2. **Grounds:** data to support the claim.
3. **Warrant:** connects the grounds or data to the claim; usually implicit, and based on appeals to ethos, pathos, or values.
4. **Backing:** further support of the warrant.
5. **Qualifier:** limits how universal the claim might be.
6. **Rebuttal:** an attempt to preempt counterarguments.

A simple example:

1. **Claim:** Presidents should hold weekly open White House press conferences.
2. **Grounds:** Press conferences enable the public to understand the president's policies and mindset.

3. **Warrant:** The public wants to know the president as best it can.
4. **Backing:** Executive communication is vital for strong democracy.
5. **Qualifier:** In times of national crisis, a regularly scheduled press conference may be inappropriate.
6. **Rebuttal:** When not at the White House, presidents can hold the scheduled press conference through a webcast.

With some practice, most students and citizens can learn these steps in making a persuasive claim. If it were taught as early as the sixth or seventh grade, everyone would have at least one powerful tool for engaging in strong public discourse on most subjects.

It is easy to see how a simple scheme for teaching argument might be presented in a classroom, long before college. Teachers could be trained in this sort of argument theory in part through the multiplicity of Web sites on the topic, and students typically find these sorts of lessons to be highly engaging. There is substantial writing on "teaching the conflicts" and the pedagogy of argument, but one of the leaders has long been Gerald Graff. He yearns for more argument throughout the curriculum and as part of life, for that matter. Graff writes:

In giving priority to ideas and arguments . . . I don't minimize the importance of qualities that can't be reduced to pure rationality—emotional intelligence, moral character, visual and aesthetic sensitivity, and creativity in storytelling and personal narrative. What I do claim is that training in these qualities will be incomplete if students are unable to translate them into persuasive public discourse. To call attention to the educational importance of visual literacy and the body you have to make arguments, not just wave pictures, do a dance, or give hugs.[20]

As Graff and others have demonstrated through their work, even in high schools students find argument to be interesting and fun. They learn more, these scholars argue, and so faculty across grades and disciplines should use available tools to teach the use of argument, for success not only in school but also in life.[21]

Barriers to training teachers in argumentation are not daunting, even with the pressures most public schools are under with regard to student performance. Rampant standardized testing dictates much of what teachers must teach, whatever produces strong achievement on high-stakes exams. But, as scholars like Graff, Brooke Noel Moore, Richard Parker, Lewis Vaughn, and others influence the professoriate, particularly in colleges of education—likely the most efficient way to train a cohort of teachers in argument—the possibility of achieving widespread competency in argumentation is real. Web resources help immensely. There are also several foundations devoted to the study and encouragement of citizen participation, such as the Kettering Foundation. A movement devoted to teaching argument that was combined with programs and organizations focused on community dialogue and participation could sow seeds for the eventual development of a culture of argument.[22]

Teaching basic argumentation skills in a classroom or in a bounded community, as well as practicing these skills, is straightforward, but the audiences are either captive or willingly engaged in social discourse. The larger challenge is in scaling up, and as we move to broader mediated and Internet arenas for talk, there are tremendous experiential changes. Some scholars have begun to take on the challenge of moving debate and argumentation to the Internet, working within communities to pursue synchronous or asynchronous debate and discussion.[23] An increasing number of teachers— cited in the notes to this book—have been introducing techniques that enable dialogue of the more rigorous and organized type that Toulmin had in mind for persuasive argumentation. In these experiments, instructors find students to be very engaged. Gatekeepers of political Web sites—our current-day editors—can organize similar sorts of debates even without grading as a goal. Setting up more structured debate channels for Internet audiences might take some concerted attention on the part of at least one editor at a site, but the discussions would add up to far more than the current discourse on even the most prominent Web sites. And the site's owners would need to figure out how to monetize this effort, to make it worth their while, with regard to audience size and profits. News and political talk sites struggle mightily with these matters now, and they will continue to do so in a Web world where old models of advertising as a source of revenue have been nearly obliterated. In the meantime, foundations devoted to argument and citizenship would be a source of support. But given the popularity of argument-style television programs—on MSNBC or Fox—there is clearly great potential to make money through argument. Why can't these arguments simply be more rule-based and rationally monitored?

Let us take, as an example, the highly successful Daily Kos, a left-leaning political Web site that has set a stylistic template for many sites across the ideological spectrum. Instead of publishing comments, from the banal to highly intelligent, as a list, wouldn't the occasional structured debate be more gratifying to readers? Editors at such sites could ask for claims, Toulmin-style, publish those, then seek warrants, and so forth. But the most obvious place to start for any editor, no matter how junior, is with "grounds" (Toulmin's step 2, in his six-stage argument). Why not press contributors for evidence and even sources for their evidence? How does it stand up to critique by others writing in or in the eyes of the editor? Is it persuasive? How so?

When contributors are pressed for evidence, data, and arguments, and these dialogues are strung together—over a series of hours or days—the sophistication level of the discourse would be far greater than the somewhat random streams of discussion we typically see in answer to a column or news item. Reading down a list of claims and warrants sent in, with participants trying their hand at contributing argument where they see fit, would be an astoundingly different experience than reading the typical chain of reaction one sees.

Another example is this CNN chain of comments, posted in July 2009, in reaction to CNN's *Political Ticker*—brief news stories of the moment, this one on President Obama's attempts at health care reform legislative action.[24] Each writer to the *Ticker* is identified by name (I have put them in italics) followed by the time they wrote in:

*Anne-Marie*

July 18, 2009, 7:57 P.M. ET

Dear God, I read your comments and you are all a big bunch of cry-babies. Did you really think that everything was going to be perfect after 6 months . . .

I'm an atheist but I least I recognize that you all, with your fake religious beliefs, have absolutely no faith in anyone except in the almighty dollar. This will be your downfall in the end.

*T Mckinley*

July 18, 2009, 7:57 P.M. ET

How can I become a filthy rich big insurance or big pharma CEO?

I want to be one of the very few who will be able to afford a private, free-market, consumer-based health care plan in a few years if we don't succeed in passing health care reform.

*Common Sense*

July 18, 2009, 7:55 P.M. ET

Aren't our representatives elected to represent us, the constituents? Putting pressure on them to vote the party line gives us taxation without representation. They need to listen to their voters, not Nancy Pelosi. She is nutty as a fruitcake anyway.

She needs to go while we still have a country that is not in full revolution.

*skip*

July 18, 2009, 7:53 P.M. ET

E.C.Coleman,

Whoa, I think it's time for your meds.

Maybe when President Obama and the other Democrats get this health care bill passed, you'll finally be able to get the help you so obviously need.

Until then, I suggest you get lots of rest. It will be okay. Really it will.

*T Mckinley*

July 18, 2009, 7:52 P.M. ET

Hey dittoheads, I have news for you. You are paying too much for the private, free-market, consumer-based health care plan that you have right now, and may be dropped from in the future when you can no longer afford it.

And guess what? The CEOs who are running these consumer-raping health care plans are laughing themselves all the way to the bank with everyone's $$$$$$$$$$$$$.

Several of these writers may be thoughtful contributors, and all were engaged enough to send comments to the CNN.com Web site. But is this typical string of political comments the best that we can hope for with Internet dialogue? Of course, there are more intelligent and even insightful strands of discourse to be found on political and news Web sites, with many contributors even producing brilliant analyses. But on the whole, this disorganized blurting out of ideas and opinions simply does not lead anywhere. People may

the highest-
st news team
to influence
rs. They have


is one step in
d taking them
ortant. Listen-
el of etiquette,
ructively. Cer-
s for behavior:
all asleep, or to


ion is another
the structured
ey can dismiss
ng: If someone
structions, their
these mechan-
better culture of


attractive path
have worked to
iety of talk pro-
lthough the fail-
Many ideological
p their advertis-
g to the bulk of
nded people seek
eir views, so they
tional attempt to

d find them intriguing.[25] But it
maker would gain much from
ientation needed to create better

on look like, on a site like the
it, with some brief training in
is string of comments into a
ficulty, although it would take
he part of the network. A jour-
uld simply push contributors
ce, and logic: "What do you
Did you see our program yes-
it an opposing view?" If this
moderator to *teach* partici-
pportive teacher-type voice is
hese days, most good report-
portive of a productive pub-
ould enable a moderator of
ie discussion, just as it does
king it more interesting and
lar contributors would start
n each other, as students do
is expected.

ing up a structure, either
—and asking that people
nent of time, money, and
necessary, and there is a
may be a short-term price
olvement (CNN, like any
naximum participation).
ghtened, and quickly. A
iight actually make a dif-
rgument culture. A vari-
if CNN—and we shall

take their advertising at face value—hopes to achieve
quality public communication about politics as "the be
on television," they would do well to innovate and try
Internet dialogue among their valued viewers and reade
the floor, and they have our attention.

## Influencing the Future of Civility: Listening

Better articulating one's claim and engaging in debate
the pursuit of civility. But hearing these arguments an
seriously, engaging in "hard listening," is equally imp
ing to in-person argumentation demands a certain lev
regardless of whether the conversation ends up const
tainly in a classroom or town meeting there are norm
It is generally unacceptable to interrupt too often, to f
leave in disgust.

The world of mediated and online argumentat
story altogether. If political Web site editors engage i
argumentation discussed in the previous section, th
arguments and evidence that reveal a lack of listeni
has not read or processed the previous remarks or ins
contributions can be rejected. But can we get past
ics and think more broadly about how to become a l
listeners?

While "hard listening" in policy debate seems a
to pursue, not many in the journalistic community
achieve the goal of better listening. There are a va
gram hosts who fail or succeed with on-air callers, a
ures seem far more pervasive than the successes. M
hosts are seeking to maintain high ratings and ke
ing revenue flowing, a purpose that demands playi
listeners. As partisan radio hosts well know, like-m
them out for entertainment and reinforcement of th
need to deliver what the audience came for. This ra

hold listeners leads to the sort of talk radio we deplore—it rarely feels like a fair fight when a caller tries to persuade a highly ideological host. I am not arguing for the elimination of such programs, as they are entertaining and they boost engagement, if not always of the very best sort. All that said, however, even in the midst of a highly ideological program like Keith Olbermann's, there are many moments during these programs where arguments of a better sort appear, if briefly. Academics, public officials, visionary journalists, and citizens, however, are the ones who need to display interest in the more substantive arguments, or they will not flourish.

What we need are more projects, national in scope like Kettering's support of the National Issues Forum or the Ford Foundation's Difficult Dialogue initiative, which is concerned with race relations. Even broader in scale and ambition is the project, StoryCorps, funded in part by the Corporation for Public Broadcasting. Started in 2003, StoryCorps is a nonprofit organization that sets up recording booths for Americans across the nation to share their life stories and worldviews, through either stationary studios or mobile units that park in communities. At this writing, more than 50,000 Americans—of all ethnicities, ages, and social classes—have visited the studios to have their conversations recorded. These stories are archived in the Library of Congress, and some are played during a weekly segment on National Public Radio. The mission is

> to honor and celebrate one another's lives through listening. We accomplish this by providing access both to the StoryCorps interview experience and to the content that emerges from these interviews.
>
> StoryCorps reminds us of the importance of listening to and learning from those around us. It celebrates our shared humanity. It tells people that their lives matter and they won't be forgotten.
>
> Through StoryCorps, we hope to create a kinder, more thoughtful and compassionate nation.

In the coming years, we will bring StoryCorps to as many people as possible, while always adhering to the highest standards of excellence. We hope to build StoryCorps into an enduring American institution.[27]

An ambitious initiative, StoryCorps has developed partnerships with universities, the Smithsonian, and a range of institutions that hope to further its goals. While political discourse occurs in many, many of the conversations among citizens who find their way to StoryCorps booths, the intention is not to encourage partisan debate about policy or electoral politics. However, the model itself is instructive and could easily be applied to a project in more focused political listening and exchange. These initiatives demand leadership and funds, and a goal of public service. But the underlying effort to teach Americans how to listen is profoundly important and ambitious. Best of all, it fits neatly with the project of sharpening citizen argumentation skills and the goal of spreading strategic civility. Civility demands dialogue—talking and listening—and so projects on the model of StoryCorps get right to the heart of interactivity and respectful community.

StoryCorps is a particularly successful venture, but it does involve equipment and professionals, since people talk with each other in booths designed to record sound properly. A large number of Americans have participated or heard recordings on their National Public Radio stations, but this is still a tiny segment of the population. How does one "scale up" such a project, so that its techniques and goals might be spread across an entire nation? The most direct route would be to adopt talking/listening models in elementary, middle, and high schools, and to capitalize on the fact that young people in the United States already love to record and post all manner of things. A program where students learn to talk and listen, and record these conversations for their own personal or school Web sites, can be engaging and empowering. A visionary high school teacher, a principal, a superintendent, or a group of parents could introduce the basics of StoryCorps into any school, setting up "model listening" for students. Thanks to the diffusion of personal recording devices, it would be quite easy, if school leaders have the imagination and desire necessary to teach young people how to talk, argue, and listen.

Anyone who tunes in to talk radio, watches television talk programs, or reads the posts on mainstream blogs like CNN or more specialized, partisan Web sites knows that we are not a great nation of listeners. Many scholars have bemoaned an American attention span shortened by the segmented media portions we are fed, and by our increasing desire for the most flashy and entertaining programming.[28] They point to the thirty-minute network newscasts, the short segments on any one topic on the network news and cable news channels, the often comical need to create drama and visual interest, and other techniques meant to keep us watching. Political speeches and debates in the United States were far longer in the nineteenth century and well into the twentieth century.

I am not arguing that our shortened attention span can be reversed. Few citizens have the time or inclination to spend a day driving to a political rally to hear speeches or debates. Instead, I propose that we use arguing and listening to build political communication skills, no matter the length of any one encounter. Projects like online debate and StoryCorps may demand more thinking and listening, but they need not be extended or dull. Far from it, reciprocity of exchange tends to excite and involve students and adults, something that has become increasingly clear to scholars of learning.[29]

## Civility and Public Opinion

We measure citizens' opinions through surveys, focus groups, and the analysis of voting behavior. But we should also be attentive to what comes *before* the expression of opinion, often called the "political socialization" process. A variety of public opinion scholars have studied the effects of media or elite cues on the development of our opinions. But the texture of fluid discussions—the continuing argument with our colleagues about health care reform or the evolving discourse on our favorite political Web sites—gets far less attention in the study of American politics. How might our study of political socialization—how children learn citizenship—be more closely linked with the nature of adult political dialogue and debate? We should tie these areas of inquiry together and see political dialogue itself as a skill that must be developed over a life span.

As I have argued elsewhere, pre-election polling (the horse race polls) is now a 24/7 sport in presidential election campaigns, and those polls in fact keep up with reality. But despite the successes of polls tracking candidate preferences, we would be hard pressed to argue that we can map *policy attitudes* in the same fashion. Good surveying on the complex issues of our time—energy, health care, economic recovery—takes time and money. No for-profit organization or university enclave can track public attitudes through surveying with the sort of speed and constancy that we might like. But one can track the evolution of attitudes by more analytical attention to political discourse on the Internet—bloggers, contributors to the *Political Ticker*, and so forth. I would posit that the Internet—in addition to polls and television talk programming—is our consistent, indeed poundingly loud, vox populi. We need new techniques for studying the variable and relentlessly moving discourse of the Internet, and my hope is that the next generation of political communication scholars will do just that.[30]

If we start to broaden our definition of "public opinion," enhancing the results of single-moment, aggregation methods (polls, elections) to include conversation and debate, we will get a fuller picture of American political culture. Can we think of "public opinion" as the full range of dialogues we see around us—from the arcane conversation on a highly ideological Web site to the content of the nightly news to whatever policy polls exist? In our time, public opinion is, whether academics like it or not, *the totality of extraordinarily difficult-to-measure forms of expression*. In fact, the technological changes in communication have never presented so much challenge as they do today. Perhaps we can no longer keep up with fluid forms of public expression around us at all moments, given the speed of communication and fluidity enabled by the Web. But we can at least evaluate public expression as it looks on the Internet with rigor and consider how we might enhance it through civility tool kits.

Using our empirical cases, can we make an argument about public opinion and civility, idiosyncratic as they are? Beginning with the emotional rallies of Governor Palin, it seems clear that she stimulated anxiety within her publics and journalists. Her gender no doubt was part of this tension, but the case teaches us something about our difficulty in understanding crowds and ideologically induced emotion during campaigns. Palin brought us face-to-face with what can be viewed as an incredibly frightening aspect of public opinion, wild contagion that can lead to non-normative and even ugly thought and behavior. But I posit that Palin's case is productive as well; passion does underlie political opinions, and well it should. The demonstration of those passions was not always laudable, but the combination of civil and uncivil discourse at her rallies, the bonding of her audiences, and their seeming volatility remind us that the texture of public opinion is of utmost import. Public opinion is not just about numbers, and civility is a window through which we can understand its texture.

President Obama pleaded with his audience at Notre Dame, asking them to help him develop new norms for civility and implicitly defining public opinion as a cohesive American whole. He sees conflict and debate as an inherent aspect of the polity. Citizens may be divided about an issue like abortion, but they still exist as a singular body, and it is civility that *makes the American public a public*. Finally, our students of Chapter 4, as troubled as they are about engaging in political discourse, are learning to be citizens. But they may be learning the wrong lessons on our campuses, fearful to participate and aggravated when they do. Problems of civility make them skeptical about being part of the public Obama desperately wants them to join. The appreciative audience at Notre Dame seems a departure from student opinion as I found it. It was a moment of engagement, respect, and tranquility, something that does not quite describe student-to-student conversation about politics on the ground at many institutions of higher learning.

In closing, while this book is not a treatise on democracy, civility is obviously a central concern to democracy. Strategic uses of civility and incivility are not inherently bad or good for its practice. Do we want more civil talk than uncivil talk? Of course. But what we need to focus on is how both civility and incivility are structured, contained, and used as "teachable moments." Even some incivility can move a policy debate along. Creating a culture of argument, and the thick skin that goes with it are long-term projects that will serve democracy well.

I have tried to steer researchers in my own field toward new approaches to civility, while also providing some avenues for K–12 teachers, journalists, bloggers, and political leaders to pursue civility. And at this moment, a variety of innovative, ethical individuals and organizations are doing just that. But if we are to fundamentally enhance civility in our time—using it as a weapon for engagement and progress—the agents I single out need to commit to the goal of culture of argument. The Internet, while it has made political communication messy and tremendously complex, enables a great advance in citizenship development and participation. If we pursue more sophisticated, useful public dialogues and realize our agency to do so, the next chapter in American civility will be one that harnesses technology for democracy in the very best of ways.

# Appendix I

Transcript of President Barack Obama's
Commencement Address,
University of Notre Dame,
May 17, 2009

(*Transcribed and published by the* Los Angeles Times)

THE PRESIDENT: Well, first of all, congratulations, Class of 2009. (Applause.) Congratulations to all the parents, the cousins—(applause)—the aunts, the uncles—all the people who helped to bring you to the point that you are here today. Thank you so much to Father Jenkins for that extraordinary introduction, even though you said what I want to say much more elegantly. (Laughter.) You are doing an extraordinary job as president of this extraordinary institution. (Applause.) Your continued and courageous—and contagious—commitment to honest, thoughtful dialogue is an inspiration to us all. (Applause.)

Good afternoon. To Father Hesburgh, to Notre Dame trustees, to faculty, to family: I am honored to be here today. (Applause.) And I am grateful to all of you for allowing me to be a part of your graduation.

And I also want to thank you for the honorary degree that I received. I know it has not been without controversy. I don't know if you're aware of this, but these honorary degrees are apparently pretty hard to come by. (Laughter.) So far I'm only 1 for 2 as President. (Laughter and applause.) Father Hesburgh is 150 for 150. (Laughter and applause.) I guess that's better. (Laughter.) So, Father Ted, after the ceremony, maybe you can give me some pointers to boost my average.

I also want to congratulate the Class of 2009 for all your accomplishments. And since this is Notre Dame—

AUDIENCE MEMBER: Abortion is murder! Stop killing children!

AUDIENCE: Booo!

THE PRESIDENT: That's all right. And since—

AUDIENCE: We are ND! We are ND!

AUDIENCE: Yes, we can! Yes, we can!

THE PRESIDENT: We're fine, everybody. We're following Brennan's [valedictorian E. Brennan Bollman] adage that we don't do things easily. (Laughter.) We're not going to shy away from things that are uncomfortable sometimes. (Applause.)

Now, since this is Notre Dame I think we should talk not only about your accomplishments in the classroom, but also in the competitive arena. (Laughter.) No, don't worry, I'm not going to talk about that. (Laughter.) We all know about this university's proud and storied football team, but I also hear that Notre Dame holds the largest outdoor 5-on-5 basketball tournament in the world—Bookstore Basketball. (Applause.)

Now this excites me. (Laughter.) I want to congratulate the winners of this year's tournament, a team by the name of "Hallelujah Holla Back." (Laughter and applause.) Congratulations. Well done. Though I have to say, I am personally disappointed that the "Barack O'Ballers" did not pull it out this year. (Laughter.) So next year, if you need a 6'2" forward with a decent jumper, you know where I live. (Laughter and applause.)

Every one of you should be proud of what you have achieved at this institution. One hundred and sixty-three classes of Notre Dame graduates have sat where you sit today. Some were here during years that simply rolled into the next without much notice or fanfare—periods of relative peace and prosperity that required little by way of sacrifice or struggle.

You, however, are not getting off that easy. You have a different deal. Your class has come of age at a moment of great consequence for our nation and for the world—a rare inflection point in history where the size and scope of the challenges before us require that we remake our world to renew its promise; that we align our deepest values and commitments to the demands of a new age. It's a privilege and a responsibility afforded to few generations—and a task that you're now called to fulfill.

This generation, your generation is the one that must find a path back to prosperity and decide how we respond to a global economy that left millions behind even before the most recent crisis hit—an economy where greed and short-term thinking were too often rewarded at the expense of fairness, and diligence, and an honest day's work. (Applause.)

Your generation must decide how to save God's creation from a changing climate that threatens to destroy it. Your generation must seek peace at a time when there are those who will stop at nothing to do us harm, and when weapons in the hands of a few can destroy the many. And we must find a way to reconcile our ever-shrinking world with its ever-growing diversity—diversity of thought, diversity of culture, and diversity of belief.

In short, we must find a way to live together as one human family. (Applause.)

And it's this last challenge that I'd like to talk about today, despite the fact that Father John stole all my best lines. (Laughter.) For the major threats we face in the 21st century—whether it's global recession or violent extremism; the spread of nuclear weapons or pandemic disease—these things do not discriminate. They do not recognize borders. They do not see color. They do not target specific ethnic groups.

Moreover, no one person, or religion, or nation can meet these challenges alone. Our very survival has never required greater cooperation and greater understanding among all people from all places than at this moment in history.

Unfortunately, finding that common ground—recognizing that our fates are tied up, as Dr. King said, in a "single garment of destiny"—is not easy. And part of the problem, of course, lies in the imperfections of man—our selfishness, our pride, our stubbornness, our acquisitiveness, our insecurities, our egos; all the cruelties large and small that those of us in the Christian tradition understand to be rooted in original sin. We too often seek advantage over others. We cling to outworn prejudice and fear those who are unfamiliar. Too many of us view life only through the lens of immediate self-interest and crass materialism; in which the world is necessarily a zero-sum game. The strong too often dominate the weak, and too many of those with wealth and with power find all manner of justification for their own privilege in the face of poverty and injustice. And so, for all our technology and scientific advances, we see here in this country and around the globe violence and want and strife that would seem sadly familiar to those in ancient times.

We know these things; and hopefully one of the benefits of the wonderful education that you've received here at Notre Dame is that you've had time to consider these wrongs in the world; perhaps recognized impulses in yourself that you want to leave behind. You've grown determined, each in your own way, to right them. And yet, one of the vexing things for those of us interested in promoting greater understanding and cooperation among people is the discovery that even bringing together persons of good will, bringing together men and women of principle and purpose—even accomplishing that can be difficult.

The soldier and the lawyer may both love this country with equal passion, and yet reach very different conclusions on the specific steps needed to protect us from harm. The gay activist and the evangelical pastor may both deplore the ravages of HIV/AIDS, but find themselves unable to bridge the cultural divide that might unite their efforts. Those who speak out against stem cell research may be rooted in an admirable conviction about the sacredness of life, but so are the parents of a child with juvenile diabetes who are convinced that their son's or daughter's hardships can be relieved. (Applause.)

The question, then—the question then is how do we work through these conflicts? Is it possible for us to join hands in common effort? As citizens of a vibrant and varied democracy, how do we engage in vigorous debate? How does each of us remain firm in our principles, and fight for what we consider right, without, as Father John said, demonizing those with just as strongly held convictions on the other side?

And of course, nowhere do these questions come up more powerfully than on the issue of abortion.

As I considered the controversy surrounding my visit here, I was reminded of an encounter I had during my Senate campaign, one that I describe in a book I wrote called *The Audacity of Hope*. A few days after I won the Democratic nomination, I received an e-mail from a doctor who told me that while he voted for me in the Illinois primary, he had a serious concern that might prevent him from voting for me in the general election. He described himself as a Christian who was strongly pro-life—but that was not what was preventing him potentially from voting for me.

What bothered the doctor was an entry that my campaign staff had posted on my website—an entry that said I would fight "right-wing ideologues who want to take away a woman's right to choose." The doctor said he had assumed I was a reasonable person, he supported my policy initiatives to help the poor and to lift up our educational system, but that if I truly believed that every pro-life individual was simply an ideologue who wanted to inflict suffering on women, then I was not very reasonable. He wrote, "I do not ask at this point that you oppose abortion, only that you speak about this issue in fair-minded words." Fair-minded words.

After I read the doctor's letter, I wrote back to him and I thanked him. And I didn't change my underlying position, but I did tell my staff to change the words on my website. And I said a prayer that night that I might extend the same presumption of good faith to others that the doctor had extended to me. Because when we do that—when we open up our hearts and our minds to those who may not think precisely like we do or believe precisely what we believe—that's when we discover at least the possibility of common ground.

That's when we begin to say, "Maybe we won't agree on abortion, but we can still agree that this heart-wrenching decision for any woman is not made casually, it has both moral and spiritual dimensions.

"So let us work together to reduce the number of women seeking abortions, let's reduce unintended pregnancies. (Applause.) Let's make adoption more available. (Applause.) Let's provide care and support for women who do carry their children to term. (Applause.) Let's honor the conscience of those who disagree with abortion, and draft a sensible conscience clause, and make sure that all of our health care policies are grounded not only in sound science, but also in clear ethics, as well as respect for the equality of women." Those are things we can do. (Applause.)

Now, understand—understand, Class of 2009, I do not suggest that the debate surrounding abortion can or should go away. Because no matter how much we may want to fudge it—indeed, while we know that the views of most Americans on the subject are complex and even contradictory—the fact is that at some level, the views of the two camps are irreconcilable. Each side will continue to make its case to the public with passion and conviction. But surely we can do so without reducing those with differing views to caricature.

Open hearts. Open minds. Fair-minded words. It's a way of life that has always been the Notre Dame tradition. (Applause.) Father Hesburgh has long spoken of this institution as both a lighthouse and a crossroads. A lighthouse that stands apart, shining with the wisdom of the Catholic tradition, while the crossroads is where "differences of culture and religion and conviction can co-exist with friendship, civility, hospitality, and especially love." And I want to join him and Father John in saying how inspired I am by the maturity and responsibility with which this class has approached the debate surrounding today's ceremony. You are an example of what Notre Dame is about. (Applause.)

This tradition of cooperation and understanding is one that I learned in my own life many years ago—also with the help of the Catholic Church.

You see, I was not raised in a particularly religious household, but my mother instilled in me a sense of service and empathy that eventually led me to become a community organizer after I graduated college. And a group of Catholic churches in Chicago helped fund an organization known as the Developing Communities Project, and we worked to lift up South Side neighborhoods that had been devastated when the local steel plant closed.

And it was quite an eclectic crew—Catholic and Protestant churches, Jewish and African American organizers, working-class black, white, and Hispanic residents—all of us with different experiences, all of us with different beliefs. But all of us learned to work side by side because all of us saw in these neighborhoods other human beings who needed our help—to find jobs and improve schools. We were bound together in the service of others.

And something else happened during the time I spent in these neighborhoods—perhaps because the church folks I worked with were so welcoming and understanding; perhaps because they invited me to their services and sang with me from their hymnals; perhaps because I was really broke and they fed me. (Laughter.) Perhaps because I witnessed all of the good works their faith inspired them to perform, I found myself drawn not just to the work with the church; I was drawn to be in the church. It was through this service that I was brought to Christ.

And at the time, Cardinal Joseph Bernardin was the Archbishop of Chicago. (Applause.) For those of you too young to have known him or known of him, he was a kind and good and wise man. A saintly man. I can still remember him speaking at one of the first organizing meetings I attended on the South Side. He stood as both a lighthouse and a crossroads—unafraid to speak his mind on moral issues ranging from poverty and AIDS and abortion to the death penalty and nuclear war. And yet, he was congenial and gentle in his persuasion, always trying to bring people together, always trying to find common ground. Just before he died, a reporter asked Cardinal Bernardin about this approach to his ministry. And he said, "You can't really get on with preaching the Gospel until you've touched hearts and minds."

My heart and mind were touched by him. They were touched by the words and deeds of the men and women I worked alongside in parishes across Chicago. And I'd like to think that we touched the hearts and minds of the neighborhood families whose lives we helped change. For this, I believe, is our highest calling.

Now, you, Class of 2009, are about to enter the next phase of your life at a time of great uncertainty. You'll be called to help restore a free market that's also fair to all who are willing to work. You'll be called to seek new sources of energy that can save our planet; to give future generations the same chance that you had to receive an extraordinary education. And whether as a person drawn to public service, or simply someone who insists on being an active citizen, you will be exposed to more opinions and ideas broadcast through more means of communication than ever existed before. You'll hear talking heads scream on cable, and you'll read blogs that claim definitive knowledge, and you will watch politicians pretend they know what they're talking about. (Laughter.) Occasionally, you may have the great fortune of actually seeing important issues debated by people who do know what they're talking about—by well-intentioned people with brilliant minds and mastery of the facts. In fact, I suspect that some of you will be among those brightest stars.

And in this world of competing claims about what is right and what is true, have confidence in the values with which you've been raised and educated. Be unafraid to speak your mind when those values are at stake. Hold firm to your faith and allow it to guide you on your journey. In other words, stand as a lighthouse.

But remember, too, that you can be a crossroads. Remember, too, that the ultimate irony of faith is that it necessarily admits doubt. It's the belief in things not seen. It's beyond our capacity as human beings to know with certainty what God has planned for us or what He asks of us. And those of us who believe must trust that His wisdom is greater than our own.

And this doubt should not push us away our faith. But it should humble us. It should temper our passions, cause us to be wary of too much self-righteousness. It should compel us to remain open and curious and eager to continue the spiritual and moral debate that began for so many of you within the walls of Notre Dame. And within our vast democracy, this doubt should remind us even as we cling to our faith to persuade through reason, through an appeal whenever we can to universal rather than parochial principles, and most of all through an abiding example of good works and charity and kindness and service that moves hearts and minds.

For if there is one law that we can be most certain of, it is the law that binds people of all faiths and no faith together. It's no coincidence that it exists in Christianity and Judaism; in Islam and Hinduism; in Buddhism and humanism. It is, of course, the Golden Rule—the call to treat one another as we wish to be treated. The call to love. The call to serve. To do what we can to make a difference in the lives of those with whom we share the same brief moment on this Earth.

So many of you at Notre Dame—by the last count, upwards of 80 percent—have lived this law of love through the service you've performed at schools and hospitals; international relief agencies and local charities. Brennan is just one example of what your class has accomplished. That's incredibly impressive, a powerful testament to this institution. (Applause.)

Now you must carry the tradition forward. Make it a way of life. Because when you serve, it doesn't just improve your community, it makes you a part of your community. It breaks down walls. It fosters cooperation. And when that happens—when people set aside their differences, even for a moment, to work in common effort toward a common goal; when they struggle together, and sacrifice together, and learn from one another—then all things are possible.

After all, I stand here today, as President and as an African American, on the 55th anniversary of the day that the Supreme Court handed down the decision in *Brown v. Board of Education*. Now, *Brown* was of course the first major step in dismantling the "separate but equal" doctrine, but it would take a number of years and a nationwide movement to fully realize the dream of civil rights for all of God's children. There were freedom rides and lunch counters and billy clubs, and there was also a Civil Rights Commission appointed by President Eisenhower. It was the 12 resolutions recommended by this commission that would ultimately become law in the Civil Rights Act of 1964.

There were six members of this commission. It included five whites and one African American; Democrats and Republicans; two Southern governors, the dean of a Southern law school, a Midwestern university president, and your own Father Ted Hesburgh, President of Notre Dame. (Applause.) So they worked for two years, and at times, President Eisenhower had to intervene personally since no hotel or restaurant in the South would serve the black and white members of the commission together. And finally, when they reached an impasse in Louisiana, Father Ted flew them all to Notre Dame's retreat in Land O'Lakes, Wisconsin—(applause)—where they eventually overcame their differences and hammered out a final deal.

And years later, President Eisenhower asked Father Ted how on Earth he was able to broker an agreement between men of such different backgrounds and beliefs. And Father Ted simply said that during their first dinner in Wisconsin, they discovered they were all fishermen. (Laughter.) And so he quickly readied a boat for a twilight trip out on the lake. They fished, and they talked, and they changed the course of history.

I will not pretend that the challenges we face will be easy, or that the answers will come quickly, or that all our differences and divisions will fade happily away—because life is not that simple. It never has been.

But as you leave here today, remember the lessons of Cardinal Bernardin, of Father Hesburgh, of movements for change both large and small. Remember that each of us, endowed with the dignity possessed by all children of God, has the grace to recognize ourselves in one another; to understand that we all seek the same love of family, the same fulfillment of a life well lived. Remember that in the end, in some way we are all fishermen.

If nothing else, that knowledge should give us faith that through our collective labor, and God's providence, and our willingness to shoulder each other's burdens, America will continue on its precious journey towards that more perfect union. Congratulations, Class of 2009. May God bless you, and may God bless the United States of America. (Applause.)

# Appendix II

UNIVERSITY SYSTEM OF GEORGIA
SURVEY ON STUDENT SPEECH AND DISCUSSION

Dear [insert school here] Student,

The Survey Research Center at the University of Georgia is assisting the University System of Georgia in conducting a survey of students at University of Georgia System institutions. You have been randomly selected from students at your institution to participate in the research study. The purpose of the study is to examine how much freedom of speech students feel that they have in their daily lives at our universities.

**Your participation is very important!** It is anticipated that the survey will take no more than 10 minutes of your time.

Your participation in this survey is completely voluntary and all information that you provide will be kept strictly confidential. **Your responses will be kept confidential and will not be released in any individually identifiable form, unless otherwise required by law. Internet communications are insecure and there is a limit to the**

*Note:* Please disregard inconsistencies in question numbering and programmer prompts. This survey was administered through a Web-based format that appeared differently than printed here.

**confidentiality that can be guaranteed due to the technology itself. However once the materials are received by the researcher, standard confidentiality procedures will be employed.** You may refuse to participate or stop taking part at any time without penalty or loss of benefits to which you are otherwise entitled. Only summary data will be reported at the conclusion of the survey, and any identifying information such as your email address will be separated from the responses you provide. No risk or discomfort is anticipated from participation in the study, and you may choose not to answer any questions you don't want to answer. Although there is no direct benefit to you personally for participating in the study, others may benefit later by insuring free speech and discussion at our colleges and universities.

To begin the survey, please click on the 'START SURVEY' link below.

If you have any questions do not hesitate to ask now or at a later date. You may contact James J. Bason, Ph.D., Director of the Survey Research Center at 542-9082, jbason@uga.edu with any questions.

Thank you for the invaluable help that you are providing by participating in this research study.

Sincerely,

James J. Bason, Ph.D.
Director and Associate Research Scientist
Survey Research Center
University of Georgia
Athens, GA 30602
(706) 542-9082
E-mail: jbason@uga.edu

*Additional questions or problems regarding your rights as a research participant should be addressed to The Chairperson, Institutional Review Board, University of Georgia, 612 Boyd Graduate Studies Research Center, Athens, Georgia 30602-7411; Telephone (706) 542-3199; E-Mail Address IRB@uga.edu.*

## START SURVEY

Please answer each of the following questions about your institution. There are no right or wrong answers to any of the items.

**Q1—What is your current classification?**
1. Freshman
2. Sophomore
3. Junior
4. Senior
5. Other [SPECIFY _____]

**Q2—How many years have you studied at your current college or university (even if you departed and returned)?**

*[Please round your answer up or down to the nearest number of years.]*

_____ years

**Q3—Overall, how would you rate your academic experience so far?**
1. Excellent
2. Good
3. Fair
4. Poor
5. Too Early to Judge

**Q4.1—What is your major?**
1. Any of the Sciences, Technology, Engineering, Math, Quantitative fields, Architecture
2. Business
3. Liberal Arts, Humanities, Social Sciences
4. Education
5. Other

Q4—Approximately how many of your courses have had a discussion component, where students were encouraged to talk about course topics?

1. Many
2. A few
3. Not Very Many
4. None

Q5—Now, referring specifically to those courses which have had a discussion component, to what degree do you feel that you participate in course discussions?

| Not Very Much at All | 2 | 3 | 4 | To a Great Degree | No Opinion |
|---|---|---|---|---|---|
| ——— | ——— | ——— | ——— | ——— | ——— |

Q6—To what degree have you felt you can freely discuss important public issues when appropriate in your classes, without fear of being criticized by the professor for your opinion?

| Not Very Much at All | 2 | 3 | 4 | To a Great Degree | No Opinion |
|---|---|---|---|---|---|
| ——— | ——— | ——— | ——— | ——— | ——— |

Q7—To what degree do you feel you can freely discuss religious issues when appropriate in your classes without fear of being criticized by the professor for your opinion?

| Not Very Much at All | 2 | 3 | 4 | To a Great Degree | No Opinion |
|---|---|---|---|---|---|
| ——— | ——— | ——— | ——— | ——— | ——— |

Q8—To what degree do you feel there are a variety of student organizations representing many different political views at your institution?

| Not Very Much at All | 2 | 3 | 4 | To a Great Degree | No Opinion |
|---|---|---|---|---|---|
| ——— | ——— | ——— | ——— | ——— | ——— |

Q9—To what degree do you feel there are a variety of student organizations representing many different religious views at your institution?

| Not Very Much at All | 2 | 3 | 4 | To a Great Degree | No Opinion |
|---|---|---|---|---|---|
| ____ | ____ | ____ | ____ | ____ | ____ |

Q10—To what degree do you feel students at your institution are respectful of the political opinions of all students at your institution?

| Not Very Much at All | 2 | 3 | 4 | To a Great Degree | No Opinion |
|---|---|---|---|---|---|
| ____ | ____ | ____ | ____ | ____ | ____ |

*[Programmer: Skip Q10 if response - 3, 4, 5, or 6]*

Q11—Please explain why you feel students aren't respectful of the political opinions of others at your institution?

_____

Q12—To what degree do you feel students at your institution are respectful of the religious beliefs of others at your institution?

| Not Very Much at All | 2 | 3 | 4 | To a Great Degree | No Opinion |
|---|---|---|---|---|---|
| ____ | ____ | ____ | ____ | ____ | ____ |

*[Programmer: Skip Q10 if response = 3, 4, 5, or 6]*

Q13—Please explain why you feel students aren't respectful of the religious beliefs of others at your institution?

_____

**Q14**—In general, how active are you in student organizations at your institution?

| | | | | Not Active | No |
|---|---|---|---|---|---|
| Very Active | 2 | 3 | 4 | at All | Opinion |
| _____ | _____ | _____ | _____ | _____ | _____ |

For the next few items, please indicate your level of agreement with each statement. Then, if asked, please provide any comments in the space provided to clarify your response.

**Q15**—Professors in my classes have sometimes inappropriately presented their own political views in class.

| Strongly | | | | Strongly | Don't |
|---|---|---|---|---|---|
| Disagree | 2 | 3 | 4 | Agree | Recall |
| _____ | _____ | _____ | _____ | _____ | _____ |

*[Programmer: Skip Q16, 17, and 18, and 19 if response = 1, 2, 3, or 6]*

**Q16**—In what ways have professors presented their own political views in class ?

_____

**Q17**—About how many times has this occurred?

_____ times

**Q18**—In any of these instances, did a student try to argue if they disagreed with the professor?
1. Yes
2. No

**Q19**—What happened?

_____

Q20—Professors in my classes have sometimes inappropriately presented their own religious views in class.

| Strongly Disagree | 2 | 3 | 4 | Strongly Agree | Don't Recall |
|---|---|---|---|---|---|
| ___ | ___ | ___ | ___ | ___ | ___ |

*[Programmer: Skip Q21, 22, 23, and 24 if response = 1, 2, 3, or 6]*

Q21—In what ways have professors presented their own political views in class?

_____

Q22—About how many times has this occurred?
_____ times

Q23—In any of these instances, did a student try to argue if they disagreed with the professor?
1. Yes
2. No

Q24—What happened?

_____

Q25—My institution does a good job of offering speakers with a variety of viewpoints.

| Strongly Disagree | 2 | 3 | 4 | Strongly Agree | Don't Know |
|---|---|---|---|---|---|
| ___ | ___ | ___ | ___ | ___ | ___ |

Q31—I have personally had a class where I felt like I had to agree with the professor's personal point of view in order to get a good grade.

| Strongly Disagree | 2 | 3 | 4 | Strongly Agree | Don't Know |
|---|---|---|---|---|---|
| ___ | ___ | ___ | ___ | ___ | ___ |

*[Programmer: Skip to Q35 if response = 3, 4, 5, or 6]*

Q31.1—Was your feeling because of something specific the professor said?
1. Yes
2. No

Q31.2—Please explain.

_____

Q33—How many classes did this occur in?
_____ classes

Q34—Can you give me an example of this?

_____

The next set of questions deals with your expectations about a good classroom learning environment.

**During the current term, how much has your coursework at this college emphasized the following?**

| Very Little | 2 | 3 | 4 | Very Much | No Opinion |
|---|---|---|---|---|---|
| _____ | _____ | _____ | _____ | _____ | _____ |

Q40.1—Memorizing facts, ideas, experiences, or theory.

Q40.2—Analyzing the basic elements of any idea, experience, or theory.

Q40.3—Synthesizing and organizing ideas, information, arguments, or methods.

Q40.4—Making judgments about the value or soundness of information, arguments, or methods.

Q40.5—Applying theories or concepts to practical problems or in new situations.

Q40.6—Using information you have read or heard to perform a new skill.

Q41—How important to you is it that instructors do not challenge your personal beliefs?

| Unimportant | 2 | 3 | 4 | Very Important | Don't Know |
|---|---|---|---|---|---|
| ___ | ___ | ___ | ___ | ___ | ___ |

Q42—How important to you is it that instructors challenge your beliefs in order to introduce new ideas?

| Unimportant | 2 | 3 | 4 | Very Important | Don't Know |
|---|---|---|---|---|---|
| ___ | ___ | ___ | ___ | ___ | ___ |

Q43—How important to you is it that you always feel comfortable in the classroom?

| Unimportant | 2 | 3 | 4 | Very Important | Don't Know |
|---|---|---|---|---|---|
| ___ | ___ | ___ | ___ | ___ | ___ |

Q44—How important to you is it that you feel the excitement of being introduced to different ideas?

| Unimportant | 2 | 3 | 4 | Very Important | Don't Know |
|---|---|---|---|---|---|
| ___ | ___ | ___ | ___ | ___ | ___ |

Q45—How important to you is it that you debate different points of view with your friends?

| Unimportant | 2 | 3 | 4 | Very Important | Don't Know |
|---|---|---|---|---|---|
| ___ | ___ | ___ | ___ | ___ | ___ |

Q46—Does your campus have a free speech zone, that is, a designated place on campus where people can speak to anyone that wants to listen?
1. Yes
2. No
3. Don't Know

Q47—Do you think free speech zones serve a useful purpose?

_____

Please answer the following demographic items.

Q48—Are you male or female?
1. Male
2. Female

Q49—What is your race?
1. White (Caucasian), Non-Hispanic
2. Black (African-American), Non-Hispanic
3. Asian/Pacific Islander
4. American Indian
5. Hispanic/Latino
6. Multi-racial
7. Prefer not to answer

Q50—What is your age?
_____ years old

Q51—Would you consider yourself a:
1. Strong Republican
2. Moderate Republican
3. Weak Republican
4. Weak Democrat
5. Moderate Democrat
6. Strong Democrat
7. Independent
8. Other

**Q52—What is your religious preference?**
1. Protestant
2. Catholic
3. Jewish
4. Muslim
5. Hindu
6. None
7. Other [SPECIFY _____]
8. Choose not to Answer

**Q53—Do you consider yourself to be from an evangelical denomination?**
1. Yes
2. No

**Q54—What is your sexual orientation? Are you . . .**
1. Heterosexual
2. Homosexual
3. Bisexual
4. Transgendered
5. Other [SPECIFY _____]
6. Prefer not to answer

**Q55—What is the highest level of education either of your parents have attained?**
1. < High School Graduate
2. High School Graduate/GED
3. Some College/Technical School
4. Bachelors Degree
5. Post-Graduate/Professional Degree

That completes the survey. Thank you for your participation. The responses you have provided will be used to assess the environment in which students learn in University System of Georgia Institutions to insure that differing viewpoints are accepted and tolerated in the learning environment.

# Notes

## Chapter 1: The Powerful—if Elusive—Nature of Civility

1. Congressman Joe Wilson's remark has made him famous, a hero to many. See his outburst at http://www.huffingtonpost.com/2009/09/09/gop-rep-wilson-yells-out_n_281480.html (accessed March 25, 2010). Wilson's fundraising efforts for his 2010 congressional campaign accelerated as a result of the comment and ensuing media coverage: Ben Smith, "Wilson Breaks $1 Million," *Politico*, September 12, 2009: available at http://www.politico.com/blogs/bensmith/0909/Wilson_campaign_Fundraising_breaks_1_million_passes_Miller.html (accessed March 25, 2010).

2. One of the most useful fact-checking sites is Politifact.com, which won the 2009 Pulitzer Prize: available at http://www.politifact.com/truth-o-meter/.

3. The only useful occurrence of the phrase "strategic civility" I could locate is from an attorney's essay on using etiquette in the practice of law—in treatment of the judge, opposing counsel, and others. While perhaps helpful to attorneys, this brief essay is primarily about the importance and effectiveness of being polite. See Eugene Meehan, "Civility as a Strategy in Litigation: Using It as a Tactical Tool." Available at http://www.supremecourtlaw.ca/default_e.asp?id=77 (accessed March 25, 2010).

4. For an incident of Obama signage being stolen, see http://www.youtube.com/watch?v=ZERbqcPyfZE&feature=related (accessed March 25, 2010). There are many videos on YouTube of both Obama and McCain yard sign theft.

5. See the excellent book edited by Samantha Besson, Jose Luis Marti, and Verena Seiler, *Deliberative Democracy and Its Discontents* (Surrey, U.K.: Ashgate Publishing, 2006).

6. One of the best scholarly books on the feeling citizens seek (and sometimes get) from media is Roderick Hart's *Seducing America: How Television Charms the Modern Voter* (Thousand Oaks, CA: Sage, 1998).

7. Aristotle wrote about friendship in *The Nicomachean Ethics*, translated by Terence Irwin (Indianapolis: Hackett Publishing, 1999). Harold Innis's famous 1951 work on communication technologies and societies is *The Bias of Communication* (Toronto: University of Toronto Press, 2008). Marshall McLuhan was prolific, but his most accessible book is *Understanding Media* (New York: Signet, 1966). While times and technologies have changed, the most imaginative use of McLuhan's ideas is still Joshua Meyrowitz's bold *No Sense of Place: The Impact of Electronic Media on Social Behavior* (New York: Oxford University Press, 1985). A good place to begin the exploration of technological determinism and its problems is Langdon Winner's *Autonomous Technology: Technics-Out-of-Control as a Theme in Political Thought* (Cambridge, MA: MIT Press, 1977).

8. Virginia Sapiro, "Considering Political Civility Historically: A Case Study of the United States" (paper presented at the Annual Meeting of the International Society for Political Psychology, 1999), 2, available at http://www.sam.kau.se/ stv/ksspa/papers/sapiro_considering_political_civility_historically.pdf (accessed March 25, 2010).

9. Norbert Elias, *The History of Manners: The Civilizing Process,* vol. 1 (New York: Pantheon, 1982).

10. "Rules of Civility and Decent Behavior" (*Foundations Magazine,* n.d.), available at http://www.foundationsmag.com/pvcivility.html (accessed January 7, 2009).

11. John Kasson, *Rudeness* and *Civilization: Manners in Nineteenth-Century Urban America* (New York: Hill and Wang, 1990), 148.

12. Ibid., 156.

13. John Stuart Mill, *On Liberty,* edited by David Spitz (New York: W. W. Norton, 1975).

14. Richard Sinopoli, "Thick-Skinned Liberalism: Redefining Civility," *American Political Science Review* 89, no. 3 (1995): 614–615.

15. Mill, *On Liberty,* 51.

16. Alexis de Tocqueville, *Democracy in America,* edited by J. P. Mayer (Garden City, NY: Anchor Books, 1969), 606.

17. Ibid.

18. Ibid., 607.

19. See Ferdinand Tönnies, *Community and Society,* edited by Jose Harris (Cambridge: Cambridge University Press, 2002).

20. Ibid., 65.

21. See Jürgen Habermas, *The Structural Transformation of the Public Sphere: An Inquiry into a Category of Bourgeois Society* (Cambridge, MA: MIT Press, 1991). One avenue to learn about deliberative projects like Fishkin's and the American Democracy Project is the AASCU Web site: http://www.aascu.org/programs/adp/ (accessed March 25, 2010). See also the work of the Kettering Foundation, devoted to the improvement of democracy: available at http://www.kettering.org/ (accessed March 25, 2010).

22. One of the best articles about civility online, groundbreaking in fact, is Zizi Papacharissi, "Democracy Online: Civility, Politeness, and the Democratic Potential of Online Political Discussion Groups," *New Media and Society* 6, no. 2 (2004): 259–283. I return to her work in Chapter 5, but Papacharissi's work represents the sort of sophistication about contemporary communication technology that is critical for the future study of civility.

23. Benjamin Barber, *Strong Democracy: Participatory Politics for a New Age* (Berkeley: University of California Press, 1984), 175.

24. Heinz Eulau, "Technology and the Fear of the Politics of Civility," *Journal of Politics* 35, no. 2 (1973): 369.

25. Ibid., 371–372.

26. Amy Gutmann and Dennis Thompson, *Democracy and Disagreement* (Cambridge, MA: Belknap Press, 1996). See also Stephen Macedo, ed., *Deliberative Politics: Essays on Democracy and Disagreement* (New York: Oxford University Press, 1999).

27. Stephen Carter, *Civility: Manners, Morals and the Etiquette of Democracy* (New York: Basic, 1998). Carter's work has stimulated a variety of excellent critiques, including Randall Kennedy, "The Case against Civility," *American Prospect* (November 1, 1998), available at http://www.prospect.org/cs/articles?article=the_case_against_civility (accessed March 25, 2010).

28. Carter, *Civility*, 53.

29. See Robert Putnam, *Bowling Alone: The Collapse and Revival of American Community* (New York: Simon and Schuster, 2001). The number of books, articles, and popular essays inspired by Putnam's work is enormous, evidenced in part by a whopping nearly 11,000 citations captured by Google Scholar alone (accessed January 16, 2009). One excellent book on the subject is Nan Lin's *Social Capital: A Theory of Social Structure and Action* (Cambridge: Cambridge University Press, 2002). There is a lively dialogue in Robert Putnam, "Robert Putnam Responds," *American Prospect* 25 (March-April 1996): 26–28, available at http://www.prospect.org/cs/articles?article=unsolved_mysteries_the_tocqueville_files_311996_rp (accessed March 25, 2010).

30. Putnam, *Bowling Alone*, 143.

31. See http://www.google.com/intl/en/press/zeitgeist2008/index.html (accessed March 25, 2010).

32. There is, of course, a substantial literature in the field of sociology on this topic. One classic starting point is Talcott Parsons's essay "The School as a Social System," *Harvard Educational Review* 29 (1958): 297–318.

## Chapter 2: Sarah Palin and Her Publics

1. Dennis Peck, "Civility: A Contemporary Context for a Meaningful Historical Concept," *Sociological Inquiry, no.* 72 (2002): 363–380.

2. See Elisabeth Noelle-Neumann, *The Spiral of Silence: Public Opinion—Our Social Skin* (Chicago: University of Chicago Press, 1984). Locke's *Essay* is now available on the Internet and searchable by key word, an excellent resource. See http://arts.cuhk.edu.hk/Philosophy/Locke/echu/ (accessed March 25, 2010).

3. See Cecil Emden, *The People and the Constitution* (London: Oxford University Press, 1956).

4. Susan Herbst, *Numbered Voices: How Opinion Polling Has Shaped American Politics* (Chicago: University of Chicago Press, 1993). See also Michael McGerr, *The Decline of Popular Politics: The American North, 1865–1928* (New York: Oxford University Press, 1986).

5. Gustave Le Bon, *The Crowd: A Study of the Popular Mind* (New York: Penguin, 1960).

6. Ibid., 27.

7. See the review by Donelson Forsyth, *Group Dynamics* (Pacific Grove, CA: Brooks/Cole Publishing, 1990). Or an application of crowd dynamic theses by Robyn Lacks, Jill Gordon, and Colleen McCue, "Who, What, and When: A Descriptive Examination of Crowd Formation, Crowd Behavior, and Participation with Law Enforcement at Homicide Scenes in One City," *American Journal of Criminal Justice,* no. 30 (2005): 1–20.

8. Le Bon, *The Crowd,* 102–103.

9. See Daniel Gilbert, Susan Fiske, and Gardner Lindzey, *The Handbook of Social Psychology,* 4th ed. (New York: Oxford University Press, 1984).

10. Elias Canetti, *Crowds and Power* (New York: Farrar, Straus, and Giroux, 1984). Key texts by Gabriel Tarde have been translated, but many have not been. For a review, see the 2005 volume of the *New Encyclopedia International Journal of Criminology* (2).

11. The Palin RNC convention speech, September 3, 2008, can be found at many Web sites, including this one with video and transcript: http://www.huffingtonpost.com/2008/09/03/sarah-palin-rnc-conventio_n_123703.html (accessed March 25, 2010).

12. "Palin Speech Gets Rave Reviews," September 4, 2008, available at http://www.usnews.com/usnews/politics/bulletin/bulletin_080904.htm (accessed March 25, 2010).

13. See the Technorati site at http://technorati.com/blogs/top100/ (accessed March 25, 2010).

14. "Internet Now Major Source of Campaign News: Continuing Partisan Divide in Cable TV News Audience," available at http://people-press.org/report/467/internet-campaign-news (accessed March 25, 2010). Before the emergence of the 24/7 cable news cycle, the Internet, and the many options for keyword searching of news venues, gathering content to analyze was expensive but not particularly difficult: Transcripts of the nightly news and a static daily paper made our "population" of news reports tidy and bounded, just as the U.S. population stays stable enough for a pollster to sample accurately at any given moment. These days of a nicely limited media discourse to sample from are now over with the fluidity of international thought on the Internet. But we can still dip into the news systematically, keeping in mind that news outlets cannot be represented as neatly as they were twenty years ago. My sample for close reading contained 175 news reports describing Governor Palin's interaction with crowds during the period from August 29 through November 30, 2008. While I searched for Palin rallies in the coverage, the nature of CNN reporting, in particular, often moves from candidate to candidate. So there were reports of Obama rallies often serially arranged with Palin's, divided by commercial breaks, although rallies were—unfortunately—rarely compared, as I note subsequently.

15. Fox News Network, *The Beltway Boys*, October 18, 2008.

16. *Fox News Sunday*, "Examining the Election and Economic Crisis," October 12, 2008.

17. *CNN Saturday Morning News*, October 18, 2008.

18. *CNN Newsroom*, October 11, 2008.

19. Julie Bosman, "Palin Plays to Conservative Base in Florida Rallies," *New York Times*, October 8, 2008, p. 22.

20. CNN Election Center, October 13, 2008.

21. Julie Bosman, "'Hussein' Chant at Palin Rally," *New York Times*, November 1, 2008, available at http://thecaucus.blogs.nytimes.com/2008/11/01/hussein-chant-at-palin-rally/ (accessed March 25, 2010).

22. John Broder and Julie Bosman, "In States Once Reliably Red, Palin and Biden Tighten Their Stump Speeches," *New York Times*, November 3, 2008, p. 18.

23. See Andrew Seder, "Secret Service Says 'Kill Him' Allegation Unfounded," *Times Leader*, October 17, 2008, available at http://www.timesleader.com/news/breakingnews/Secret_Service_says_Kill_him_allegation_unfounded_.html (accessed March 25, 2010).

24. Michelle Malkin, "Massive Crowds, Missing MSM," September 10, 2008, available at http://michellemalkin.com/2008/09/10/massive-crowds-missing-msm/ (accessed March 25, 2010).

25. "The McCain-Palin Mob in Strongsville, Ohio," October 8, 2008, available at http://bloggerinterrupted.com/2008/10/video-the-mccain-palin-mob-in-strongsville-ohio (accessed March 25, 2010).

26. Andrew Sullivan, "Next Up: A CGI Palin," October 21, 2008, available at http://andrewsullivan.theatlantic.com/the_daily_dish/2008/10/palin-as-dean.html (accessed March 25, 2010).

27. The *Washington Post* tracked candidate rallies through the fall of 2008. They report dates and locations of many candidate stops, and so this is a useful archive. Yet as they note, it does not include all candidate stops or remarks, such as private fundraising events. See http://projects.washingtonpost.com/2008-presidential-candidates/tracker/candidates/sarah-palin/states (accessed March 25, 2010).

28. A typical story on the Bradley effect was "Will Obama Suffer from the Bradley Effect," October 14, 2008, available at http://www.cnn.com/2008/POLITICS/10/13/obama.bradley.effect/ (accessed March 25, 2010).

29. Dana Milbank, "In Fla., Palin Goes for the Rough Stuff as Audience Boos Obama," October 6, 2008, available at http://voices.washingtonpost.com/44/2008/10/06/in_fla_palin_goes_for_the_roug.html (accessed March 25, 2010).

30. The scholarly literature on the history and progress of socialism in the United States is vast. One recent book of interest is Seymour Martin Lipset and Gary Marks, *It Didn't Happen Here: Why Socialism Failed in the United States* (New York: Norton, 2001). A documentary on American socialism by James Klein and Julia Reichert, *Seeing Red* (1983), is worth consulting. It contains rare oral history footage from some of the leftist leaders in the United States who belonged to or were affiliated with the Socialist Party during its most successful twentieth-century years.

31. See "Better Ratings for Foreign Policy Than Domestic Issues," April 23, 2009, available at http://people-press.org/reports/pdf/509.pdf (accessed March 25, 2010).

32. Sarah Palin, campaign rally in Lakewood, Florida, November 3, 2008.

33. The Marietta and Columbus rallies both occurred on November 2, 2008. The rally at Bowling Green was held on October 29, 2008.

34. Susan Herbst, *Politics at the Margin: Historical Studies of Public Opinion outside the Mainstream* (New York: Cambridge University Press, 1994).

35. Joan B. Landes, *Women and the Public Sphere in the Age of the French Revolution* (Ithaca, NY: Cornell University Press, 1988), 73.

36. Mary Ryan, *Women in Public: Between Banners and Ballots, 1825–1880* (Baltimore: Johns Hopkins University Press, 1992).

37. Judith R. Walkowitz, *City of Dreadful Delight: Narratives of Sexual Danger in Late-Victorian London* (Chicago: University of Chicago Press, 1992), p. 20.

38. Kenneth Cmiel, *Democratic Eloquence: The Fight over Popular Speech in Nineteenth-Century America* (Berkeley: University of California Press, 1990), p. 70. See also Kathleen Hall Jamieson's *Eloquence in an Electronic Age* (New York: Oxford University Press, 1988). Jamieson contrasts the ways women's speech has been seen with views of male speech. Female speakers were, in centuries past, labeled whores, hysterics, and witches, among other societal threats.

39. Bonnie Erbe, "Sarah Palin's Feminist Flip-Flop," October 24, 2008, available at http://www.usnews.com/blogs/erbe/2008/10/24/sarah-palins-feminist-flip-flop.html (accessed March 25, 2010).

40. As the Huffington Post points out, Palin got the quotation wrong. The actual quotation is as follows: "There's a place in hell reserved for women who don't *help* other women." For the rally video, see http://www.huffingtonpost.com/2008/10/05/palin-misquotes-albright_n_131967.html (accessed March 25, 2010).

41. Palin and her staff were accused of overspending on clothing for Palin and her family. See Jeanne Cummings, "GOP Donors Critical of Palin's Pricey Threads," October 22, 2008, available at http://www.politico.com/news/stories/1008/14840.html (accessed March 25, 2010).

42. See Mark Leibovich, "Among Rock-Ribbed Fans of Palin, Dudes Rule," *New York Times*, October 19, 2008, p. 1.

43. There are many fine books on this subject, but one to start with is Naomi Wolf's *The Beauty Myth: How Images of Beauty Are Used against Women* (New York: Anchor, 1992).

44. Gary Kamiya, "The Dominatrix," September 9, 2008, available at http://www.salon.com/opinion/kamiya/2008/09/09/mistress_palin/ (accessed March 25, 2010).

45. We cannot know much about the willingness of the Clinton campaign to use race hatred—tapping into existing discrimination in places like rural Pennsylvania—as a tactic. Obama's problems in this regard were much more likely fueled by the publicity surrounding his former pastor in Chicago, the Reverend Jeremiah Wright. Clinton was not opposed to jumping on Obama gaffes that indirectly offended whites (e.g., his remark about how bitter Pennsylvanians "cling to guns or religion"). For more discussion, albeit limited and without conventional citation, see John Heilemann and Mark Halperin, *Game Change: Obama and the Clintons, McCain and Palin, and the Race of a Lifetime* (New York: Harper, 2010).

## Chapter 3: Barack Obama, Difference, and Civility

1. The American Presidency Project is one of the most valuable databases for the study of U.S. politics. See http://www.presidency.ucsb.edu/ (accessed March 25, 2010).

2. John Adams, "Special Message," January 8, 1799, available at http://www.presidency.ucsb.edu/ws/index.php?pid=65665&st (accessed March 25, 2010).

3. Kennedy, "Inaugural Address," January 20, 1961, available at http://www.presidency.ucsb.edu/ws/index.php?pid=8032&st (accessed March 25, 2010).

4. Gallup tracks presidential approval statistics, and has done so since the Eisenhower presidency. See http://www.gallup.com/poll/121790/Obama-Job-Approval-Trends-Downward-Second-Quarter.aspx (accessed March 25, 2010).

5. See George Edwards, *On Deaf Ears: The Limits of the Bully Pulpit* (New Haven, CT: Yale University Press, 2003); Jeffrey Tulis, *The Rhetorical Presidency* (Princeton, NJ: Princeton University Press, 1987); Carlyn Kohrs Campbell and Kathleen Hall Jamieson, *Deeds Done in Words: Presidential Rhetoric and the Genres of Governance* (Chicago: University of Chicago Press, 1990).

While I use some tools from the study of rhetoric, I am not a rhetorician. For an example of how one uses the best of contemporary rhetorical tools in understanding presidential speech, G. Thomas Goodnight's work is a wonderful place to start. See, for example, "Ronald Reagan's Reformulation of the Rhetoric of War: Analysis of the 'Zero Option,' 'Evil Empire,' and 'Star Wars' Addresses," *Quarterly Journal of Speech*, no. 72 (1986): 390–414.

6. Campbell and Jamieson, *Deeds Done in Words*, 5–6. Whether presidents move public opinion effectively or not is a question lacking a definitive answer. Some have argued that there is evidence for no effect of presidential speech making on public preferences, others argue for a moderate effect, and still others believe in profound effects, even if they are not easily measured. See Paul Quirk's succinct review of the issues, "When the President Speaks, How Do the People Respond?" *Critical Review*, no. 19 (2007): 427–446.

7. While Obama received an honorary doctorate at Notre Dame and gave the commencement address, he did not receive an honorary degree at Arizona State, an action fraught with controversy. See Adam Sneed, "Obama Won't Receive ASU Honorary Degree," *State Press*, April 8, 2008, available at http://www.statepress.com/node/5763 (accessed March 25, 2010).

8. Liz Halloran, "Obama's Notre Dame Visit Stirs Passions," *National Public Radio*, May 14, 2009, available at http://www.npr.org/templates/story/story.php?storyId=104107546 (accessed March 25, 2010).

9. Margaret Fosmoe, "In Mock Election at ND, Obama Wins Presidency," South Bend Tribune.com, October 8, 2008, available at http://www.southbendtribune.com/apps/pbcs.dll/article?AID=/20081008/NEWS07/810080315/1011/News (accessed March 25, 2010).

10. "Obama, Catholics and the Notre Dame Commencement," Pew Forum on Religion and Public Life, April 30, 2009, available at http://pewforum.org/Politics-and-Elections/Obama-Catholics-and-the-Notre-Dame-Commencement.aspx (accessed March 25, 2010).

11. See Joshua Rhett Miller, "Critics Blast Obama's Scheduled Notre Dame Commencement Address," FOXNews.com, March 24, 2009, available at http://www.foxnews.com/politics/first100days/2009/03/24/critics-blast-obamas-notre-dame-commencement-address/ (accessed March 25, 2010).

12. See Appendix I. Obama's speech to Notre Dame's graduating class, on May 17, 2009, can be viewed on a variety of Web sites. A written transcript is available at http://www.latimes.com/news/nationworld/nation/chi-barack-obama-notre-dame-speech,0,3194399,full.story (accessed March 25, 2010). Mine is not an analysis of abortion rhetoric. However, there is an excellent scholarly literature on the rhetoric of abortion, past and present. Celeste Condit is one of the leaders; see her *Decoding Abortion Rhetoric: Communicating Social Change* (Urbana: University of Illinois Press, 1994).

13. David Zarefsky, "Presidential Rhetoric and the Power of Definition," *Presidential Studies Quarterly*, no. 34 (September 2004): 612.

14. Ibid., 612.

15. Ibid., 613.

16. Arthur Bentley, *The Process of Government: A Study of Social Pressures* (Chicago: University of Chicago Press, 1908), 240. Nicholas Lemann has written a very fine article on Bentley, "Conflict of Interests," *New Yorker*, August 11, 2008. See http://www.newyorker.com/arts/critics/atlarge/2008/08/11/080811crat_atlarge_lemann (accessed March 25, 2010).

17. Herbert Blumer, "Public Opinion and Public Opinion Polling," *American Sociological Review* 13 (1948): 242–249. For an argument that Blumer is no longer relevant to academic research, see Philip Converse, "Changing Conceptions of Public Opinion in the Political Process," *Public Opinion Quarterly* 51, Supplement (1987): 12–24.

18. See Alex Mostrous, "White House Backs Right to Arms Outside Obama Events," *Washington Post*, August 19, 2009, available at http://www.washingtonpost.com/wp-dyn/content/article/2009/08/18/AR2009081803416.html?hpid=topnews (accessed March 25, 2010).

19. See http://www.youtube.com/watch?v=_kxaGfClPws (accessed March 25, 2010).

20. Adam C. Smith, "Protesters in Ybor City Drown Out Health Care Summit on Obama's Proposal," August 7, 2009, available at http://www.tampabay.com/news/politics/article1025529.ece (accessed March 25, 2010).

21. Carrie Budoff Brown, "W.H. Backs Away from Public Option," Politico, August 16, 2009, available at http://dyn.politico.com/printstory.cfm?uuid=245DC6DA-18FE-70B2-A8D1F077D528627B (accessed March 25, 2010).

22. Lori Montgomery and Perry Bacon, Jr., "Key Senator Calls for Narrower Health Reform Measure; Republican Grassley Cites Town Hall Anger,"

*Washington Post*, August 20, 2009, available at http://www.washingtonpost.com/wp-dyn/content/article/2009/08/19/AR2009081904125.html (accessed March 25, 2010).

23. Bob MacGuffie, "Rocking the Town Halls—Best Practices," Right Principles, available at http://thinkprogress.org/wp-content/uploads/2009/07/townhallactionmemo.pdf (accessed March 25, 2010).

24. See http://www.glennbeck.com/content/articles/article/198/29309/ (accessed March 25, 2010).

25. "Statement on the Current Health Care Debate," Friday, August 7, 2009, Facebook http://www.facebook.com/note.php?note_id=113851103434 (accessed March 25, 2010).

26. Ginger Adams Otis, "'We Won't Pull Plug on Granny': O Rips Mercy-Kill 'Boogeymen' in Health Town Hall," August 12, 2009, *New York Post*, available at http://www.nypost.com/seven/08122009/news/nationalnews/we_wont_pull_plug_on_granny_184093.htm (accessed March 25, 2010).

27. "A Message to Alaskans about the Stimulus Veto and the Health Care Town Halls," August 9, 2009, Facebook, http://www.facebook.com/note.php?note_id=114912353434 (accessed March 25, 2010).

28. Rachel McDonald, "Courteous Crowd Comes to Town Hall in Eugene," *Oregon Public Radio*, August 19, 2009, available at http://news.opb.org/article/5654-courteous-crowd-comes-town-hall-eugene/ (accessed March 25, 2010).

29. Michael Mason, "Flash: Barney Frank Gets Testy," *New York Times*, August 20, 2009, available at http://prescriptions.blogs.nytimes.com/2009/08/20/news-flash-barney-frank-gets-testy/ (accessed March 25, 2010).

30. Mark Jurkowitz, "Anger and Rancor Fuel Cable's Health Care Coverage," available at http://www.journalism.org/index_report/pej_news_coverage_index_august_1016_2009 (accessed March 25, 2010).

31. Pew Research Center, "Many Fault Media Coverage of Health Care Debate," August 6, 2009, available at http://people-press.org/report/533/many-fault-media-coverage-of-health-care (accessed March 25, 2010).

32. Quoted in Kyle Trygstad and Mike Momoli, "Before Friendly Crowd, Obama Urges Civility," Politics Nation, August 11, 2009, available at http://www.realclearpolitics.com/politics_nation/2009/08/before_friendly_crowd_obama_ur.html (accessed March 25, 2010).

33. Jonathan Chait, "The Obama Method," *New Republic*, July 1, 2009, available at http://www.cbsnews.com/stories/2009/06/24/opinion/main5109622.shtml (accessed March 25, 2010).

34. Sean Wilentz, "Who Lincoln Was," *New Republic*, July 15, 2009, p. 47.

## Chapter 4: Our Future Leaders: College Students and Political Argument

1. Creating a list of books and articles would be too great a task to attempt here, and they would span decades, disciplines, and levels of higher education. One recent book is a fine exemplar of the rigorous self-reflection one finds: See Rebekah Nathan, *My Freshman Year: What a Professor Learned by Becoming a Student* (Ithaca, NY: Cornell University Press, 2005).

2. A good place to begin the study of campus free speech is A. Lee Fritschler, Bruce Smith, and Jeremy Mayer's *Closed Minds? Politics and Ideology in American Universities* (Washington, DC: Brookings Institution Press, 2008).

3. See http://www.mibazaar.com/fastestgrowingstates.html (accessed March 25, 2010).

4. For details on this legislation, see http://www.georgialegislativewatch.com/2007/01/26/2007_08_hb154/ (accessed March 25, 2010).

5. "Intellectual diversity" in Georgia has been an area of concern over several years. But the state concerns reflect the national work of right, left, and center interest groups, all of whom see different (and worrisome) ideological biases on campus. Among those who worry about a liberal bias is FIRE (the Foundation for Individual Rights in Education). See Jeff Emanual, "Can Government Legislate Intellectual Diversity," March 2, 2007, available at http://www.thefire.org/index.php/article/7798.html (accessed March 25, 2010). For an opposing view, see the Web site of the organization Free Exchange on Campus, a national faculty and student organization: "Intellectual Diversity and the So-Called Academic Bill of Rights: FAQs," posted February 15, 2006, at http://www.freeexchangeoncampus.org/index.php?option=com_content&task=view&id=4&Itemid=5 (accessed March 25, 2010). On Georgia, see "Tolerant Faculty, Intolerant Students," *Inside Higher Ed*, August 20, 2008, available at http://www.insidehighered.com/news/2008/08/20/georgia (accessed March 25, 2010).

6. The full survey, the methodology, and all results are available online at http://www.usg.edu/images/news_files/student_speech_0508.pdf (accessed on March 25, 2010).

7. The response rates for 2008 and 2009 were 8.2 percent and 5.1 percent, respectively, not particularly low for a student survey on a somewhat theoretical topic (as compared to parking, fees, or food service). But, to make certain that the sample was representative of the large number of students in public universities across the state, we compared our respondent pool to the larger population on multiple dimensions: gender, race, age, student classification, and type of institution. The samples match well, although there was a negligible overrepresentation in some categories (e.g., seniors are overrepresented in 2008).

8. There were some changes from 2008 to 2009, although there is not much of a discernable pattern. Another reason to emphasize the 2008 data is that our response rate dropped in 2009, possibly because we shifted the survey period to earlier in the semester. But the changes could be due to other factors as well, including competition with other campus surveys or increased hours of work—for pay—beyond campus, resulting from the economic downturn and increased university fees.

9. Student responses are being reproduced here as submitted, with punctuation and grammatical errors left intact.

10. This is a good faculty forum devoted to literature on student apathy and tools for fighting it. See the DePaul University Teaching Commons Web site: http://teachingcommons.depaul.edu/How_to/engage_students/motivating/motivating.html (accessed March 25, 2010).

11. Given my experience with undergraduates, my sense was that asking them directly about civility or incivility as a strategic asset would have been somewhat baffling. It is a sophisticated approach, and not a frame they would normally use, even those who are politically active. Instead, I searched for more natural instances of strategic talk within the abundance of comments they made about civility on campus.

12. See James McCroskey, John Daly, and Gail Sorensen, "Personality Correlates of Communication Apprehension: A Research Note," *Human Communication Research* 3, no. 4 (2006): 376–380.

13. See http://www.csulb.edu/divisions/aa/grad_undergrad/senate/documents/Civility_Final.pdf (accessed on March 25, 2010).

14. Gerald Uelmen, "The Price of Free Speech: Campus Hate Speech Codes," available at http://www.scu.edu/ethics/publications/iie/v5n2/codes.html (accessed March 25, 2010).

## Chapter 5: Conclusion: Civility, Communication, and a Culture of Argument

1. Rep. Eric Cantor (R-VA) received a serious death threat after the March 2010 health care vote. See http://www.politico.com/news/stories/0310/35152.html (accessed March 31, 2010).

2. Raymond Williams, *Technology and Cultural Form* (London: Routledge, 2003).

3. See Kathleen Hall Jamieson, "Civility in the House of Representatives: The 106th Congress," *Report Series: The Annenberg Public Policy Center of the University of Pennsylvania*, 2001, available at http://www.annenbergpublicpolicycenter.org/Downloads/Political_Communication/106thCongressCivil/2001_civility106th.pdf (accessed March 25, 2010).

4. Kathleen Hall Jamieson, "Civility in the House of Representatives," *APPC Report* 10, March 1997, available at http://www.annenbergpublicpolicycenter.org/NewsDetails.aspx?myId=195 (accessed March 25, 2009).

5. John Locke, *An Essay Concerning Human Understanding*, edited by Alexander Campbell Fraser (Oxford: Clarendon Press, 2007).

6. Archived programs are available at http://www.pbs.org/newshour/indepth_coverage/politics/political_wrap/ (accessed March 25, 2010).

7. On incivility on television, see Diana Mutz, "Effects of 'In-Your-Face' Television Discourse on Perceptions of a Legitimate Opposition," *American Political Science Review* 101, no. 4 (2007): 621–635.

8. Wikipedia's own entry on "netiquette" is an interesting roundup of some issues: http://en.wikipedia.org/wiki/Netiquette (accessed March 25, 2010).

9. A thoughtful book on the Internet and its effects, well worth reading and written for a broad audience, is Jonathan Zittrain, *The Future of the Internet—And How to Stop It* (New Haven, CT: Yale University Press, 2009).

10. Zizi Papacharissi, "Democracy Online: Civility, Politeness, and the Democratic Potential of Online Political Discussion Groups," *New Media and Society* 6, no. 2 (2004): 259–283.

11. Ibid., 277. Perhaps the discussants toned their exchanges down because of discomfort with conflict, as we saw with students in Chapter 4.

12. Jonathan Miller, "Worth Noting; Stop the Presses (or the Web Sites)," *New York Times,* March 12, 2006, available at http://query.nytimes.com/gst/fullpage.html?res=990CE4DF1031F931A25750C0A9609C8B63 (accessed March 25, 2010).

13. Don Aucoin, "Control P's and Q's," Boston.com, February 21, 2009, available at http://www.boston.com/lifestyle/articles/2009/02/21/control_ps__qs/?page=1 (accessed March 25, 2010).

14. While most users of the Internet know this, I should mention that many popular sites are regulated for vandalism, civility content, and inaccurate information. Wikipedia is one extraordinarily popular information source, and its leaders are well aware of the challenges, as they have been since its inception. See their discussion, along with links about their efforts, at http://en.wikipedia.org/wiki/Reliability_of_Wikipedia (accessed March 25, 2010). Like most sites, even the Wikipedia page on their own accuracy should be viewed with a critical eye!

15. See Tim Rutten, "Incivility Is Taking the Place of Facts," *Denver Post,* September 25, 2009, available at http://www.denverpost.com/news/ci_13415748 (accessed March 25, 2010).

16. The Commission on Presidential Debates Web site is http://www.debates.org/ (accessed on March 25, 2010).

17. See http://blog.nielsen.com/nielsenwire/tag/presidential-debate/ (accessed on March 25, 2010).

18. The phrase "culture of argument" was most famously used first by James Boyd White in his *When Words Lose Their Meaning: Constitutions and Reconstitutions of Language, Character, and Community* (Chicago: University of Chicago Press, 1985). He uses the phrase to describe the social word or language of the law, a humanistic inquiry into the nature of legal and constitutional augmentation. This is important work, well worth studying. However, I use "culture of argument" in a different and less technical and indeed less sophisticated fashion, even if I am indebted to White for the phrase.

19. See Stephen Toulmin, *The Uses of Argument* (Cambridge: Cambridge University Press, 1969).

20. Gerald Graff, *Clueless in Academe: How Schooling Obscures the Life of the Mind* (New Haven, CT: Yale University Press, 2004).

21. One example of a rich resource for teachers is the Web site of IDEA, the International Debate Education Association: http://www.idebate.org/about/training.php (accessed March 25, 2010).

22. There are a variety of excellent books on argumentation and how it can be taught. See, for example, Brooke Noel Moore and Richard Parker, *Critical Thinking* (New York: McGraw-Hill, 2008), or Lewis Vaughn, *The Power of Critical Thinking: Effective Reasoning about Ordinary and Extraordinary Claims* (New York: Oxford University Press, 2007).

23. Sites like these are an enormous contribution to American pedagogy. See the University of Virginia Curry School of Education tools for teaching online debate: http://onlinelearn.edschool.virginia.edu/debate/facil.html# (accessed March 25, 2010). An excellent experimental path by Shawn Love is very promising as well. See his "Online Debate: A Case Study Combining Traditional Strategy and Online Technology," available at http://www.itdl.org/Journal/Sep_04/article06.htm (accessed on March 25, 2010). Enterprising students at the University of Wisconsin have created a less formal way to teach and encourage debate called the Great Political Debate; it is well worth visiting. See http://www.thegpd.com/ (accessed March 25, 2010).

24. See http://politicalticker.blogs.cnn.com/2009/07/18/obama-political-team-turns-its-sights-on-house-dems/#comments (accessed March 25, 2010).

25. It is impossible to document the number of people reading, of course. But as noted previously, Technocrati is one excellent source one can use to get a sense of site popularity. The CNN *Political Ticker* ranks very high in Technocrati's top one hundred Web sites, twelfth at this writing. See http://technorati.com/blogs/top100/ (accessed March 25, 2010).

26. There are alternatives to Toulmin's model and approach, of course. See Moore and Parker, *Critical Thinking*, or Vaughn, *The Power of Critical Thinking*.

27. See http://storycorps.org/about (accessed March 25, 2010).

28. These arguments about shortened American attention spans began in earnest with Neil Postman's *Amusing Ourselves to Death: Public Discourse in the Age of Show Business* (New York: Penguin, 1986). For a more recent perspective, see Peter Nardulli, *Domestic Perspectives on Contemporary Democracy* (Urbana, IL: University of Illinois Press, 2008).

29. This has become a large literature, stretching from studies of argument to those seeking to understand the effects of cognitive and emotional involvement on learning and opinion change. To start, see, for example, E. Michael Nussbaum and Gale Sinatra, "Argument and Conceptual Engagement," *Contemporary Educational Psychology*, no. 28 (2003): 384–395. See also the broad collection edited by David Dai and Robert Sternberg, *Motivation, Emotion, and Cognition: Integrative Perspectives on Intellectual Functioning and Development* (Mahwah, NJ: Lawrence Erlbaum, 2004).

30. See Susan Herbst, "Public Opinion—Re-visited," *Breaux Symposium*, October, 17, 2009 (unpublished manuscript, available from the author).

# Bibliography

Adams, John. "Special Message." American Presidency Project, January 8, 1799. Available at http://www.presidency.ucsb.edu/ws/index.php?pid=65665&st (accessed March 25, 2010).

American Democracy Project. American Association of State Colleges and Universities. Available at http://www.aascu.org/programs/adp/ (accessed March 25, 2010).

Aristotle. *The Nicomachean Ethics*. Trans. Terence Irwin. Indianapolis: Hackett Publishing, 1999.

Aucoin, Don. "Control P's and Q's." Boston.com, February 21, 2009. Available at http://www.boston.com/lifestyle/articles/2009/02/21/control_ps__qs/?page=1 (accessed March 25, 2010).

Barber, Benjamin. 1984. *Strong Democracy: Participatory Politics for a New Age*. Berkeley: University of California Press, 1984.

Bentley, Arthur. *The Process of Government: A Study of Social Pressures*. Chicago: University of Chicago Press, 1908.

Besson, Samantha, Jose L. Marti, and Verena Seiler. *Deliberative Democracy and Its Discontents*. Surrey: Ashgate Publishing, 2006.

Blumer, Herbert. "Public Opinion and Public Opinion Polling." *American Sociological Review* 13 (1948): 242–249.

Bosman, Julie. "'Hussein' Chant at Palin Rally." *New York Times*, November 1, 2008. Available at http://thecaucus.blogs.nytimes.com/2008/11/01/hussein-chant-at-palin-rally/ (accessed March 25, 2010).

————. "Palin Plays to Conservative Base in Florida Rallies." *New York Times*, October 8, 2008.

Broder, John, and Julie Bosman. "In States Once Reliably Red, Palin and Biden Tighten Their Stump Speeches." *New York Times*, November 3, 2008.

Brown, Carrie B. "W.H. Backs Away from Public Option." Politico, August 16, 2009. Available at http://dyn.politico.com/printstory.cfm?uuid=245DC6DA-18FE-70B2-A8D1F077D528627B (accessed March 25, 2010).

Campbell, Carlyn K., and Kathleen H. Jamieson. *Deeds Done in Words: Presidential Rhetoric and the Genres of Governance*. Chicago: University of Chicago Press, 1990.

"Campus Civility and the Disruption of Learning: A Guide for Faculty and Staff." California State University: Long Beach. Available at http://www.csulb.edu/divisions/aa/grad_undergrad/senate/documents/Civility_Final.pdf (accessed March 25, 2010).

Canetti, Elias. *Crowds and Power*. New York: Farrar, Straus, and Giroux, 1984.

Carter, Stephen. *Civility: Manners, Morals and the Etiquette of Democracy*. New York: Basic, 1998.

"Caught on Video: Stealing an Obama Sign." YouTube, October 18, 2008. Available at http://www.youtube.com/watch?v=ZERbqcPyfZE&feature=related (accessed March 25, 2010).

Chait, Jonathan. "The Obama Method." *New Republic*, July 1, 2009. Available at http://www.cbsnews.com/stories/2009/06/24/opinion/main5109622.shtml (accessed March 25, 2010).

Cmiel, Kenneth. *Democratic Eloquence: The Fight over Popular Speech in Nineteenth Century America*. Berkeley: University of California Press, 1990.

CNN. CNN Election Center. October 13, 2008.

————. *CNN Newsroom*. October 11, 2008.

————. *CNN Saturday Morning News*. October 18, 2008.

CNN Politics.com. "Obama Political Team Turns Its Sights on House Dems." July 18, 2008. Available at http://politicalticker.blogs.cnn.com/2009/07/18/obama-political-team-turns-its-sights-on-house-dems/#comments (accessed March 25, 2010).

————. "Will Obama Suffer from the Bradley Effect?" October 14, 2008. Available at http://www.cnn.com/2008/POLITICS/10/13/obama.bradley.effect/ (accessed March 25, 2010).

Commission on Presidential Debates. 2008. Available at http://www.debates.org/ (accessed March 25, 2010).

Condit, Celeste. *Decoding Abortion Rhetoric: Communicating Social Change*. Urbana: University of Illinois Press, 1994.

Converse, Philip. "Changing Conceptions of Public Opinion in the Political Process." *Public Opinion Quarterly* 51, Supplement (1987): 12–24.

Cummings, Jeanne. "GOP Donors Critical of Palin's Pricey Threads." Politico, October 22, 2008. Available at http://www.politico.com/news/stories/1008/14840.html (accessed March 25, 2010).

Dai, David, and Robert Sternberg, eds. *Motivation, Emotion, and Cognition: Integrative Perspectives on Intellectual Functioning and Development*. Mahwah, NJ: Lawrence Erlbaum, 2004.

Edwards, George. *On Deaf Ears: The Limits of the Bully Pulpit*. New Haven, CT: Yale University Press, 2003.

Elias, Norbert. *The History of Manners: The Civilizing Process*, vol. 1. New York: Pantheon, 1982.

Emanual, Jeff. "Can Government Legislate Intellectual Diversity." FIRE, March 2, 2007. Available at http://www.thefire.org/index.php/article/7798.html (accessed March 25, 2010).

Emden, Cecil. *The People and the Constitution*. London: Oxford University Press, 1956.

Epstein, Keith. "McCain's VP Choice: 'Sarah Barracuda.'" *Business Week*, August 29, 2008. Available at http://www.businessweek.com/election/2008/blog/archives/2008/08/mccains_vp_choi.html (accessed March 25, 2010).

Erbe, Bonnie. "Sarah Palin's Feminist Flip-Flop." USNews.com, October 24, 2008. Available at http://www.usnews.com/blogs/erbe/2008/10/24/sarah-palins-feminist-flip-flop.html (accessed March 25, 2010).

Eulau, Heinz. "Technology and the Fear of the Politics of Civility." *Journal of Politics* 35, no. 2 (1973): 369, 371–372.

"Facilitating Debate." OnlineLearn: Designing Learning Communities. November 2002. Available at http://onlinelearn.edschool.virginia.edu/debate/facil.html# (accessed March 25, 2010).

Forsyth, Donelson. *Group Dynamics*. Pacific Grove, CA: Brooks/Cole Publishing, 1990.

Fosmoe, Margaret. "In Mock Election at ND, Obama Wins Presidency." South Bend Tribune.com, October 8, 2008. Available at http://www.southbendtribune.com/apps/pbcs.dll/article?AID=/20081008/NEWS07/810080315/1011/News (accessed March 25, 2010).

*Foundations Magazine*. "Rules of Civility and Decent Behavior." Available at http://www.foundationsmag.com/pvcivility.html (accessed March 25, 2010).

Fox News Network. "The Beltway Boys." October 18, 2008.

*Fox News Sunday*. "Examining the Election and Economic Crisis." October 12, 2008.

Free Exchange on Campus. "Intellectual Diversity and the So-called Academic Bill of Rights: FAQs." February 15, 2006. Available at http://www.freeexchangeoncampus.org/index.php?option=com_content&task=view&id=4&Itemid=5 (accessed March 25, 2010).

Fritschler, Lee, Bruce Smith, and Jeremy Mayer. *Closed Minds? Politics and Ideology in American Universities.* Washington, DC: Brookings Institution Press, 2008.

Gallup. "Obama Job Approval Trends Downward in Second Quarter." July 20, 2009. Available at http://www.gallup.com/poll/121790/Obama-Job-Approval-Trends-Downward-Second-Quarter.aspx (accessed March 25, 2010).

Georgia Legislative Watch. HB 154—Intellectual Diversity in Higher Education Act. January 26, 2007. Available at http://www.georgialegislativewatch.com/2007/01/26/2007_08_hb154/ (accessed March 25, 2010).

Gilbert, Daniel, Susan Fiske, and Gardner Lindzey. *The Handbook of Social Psychology,* 4th ed. New York: Oxford University Press, 1984.

"Glenn Beck: Find Your Voice." The Glenn Beck Program. August 12, 2009. Available at http://www.glennbeck.com/content/articles/article/198/29309/ (accessed March 25, 2010).

Goodnight, G. Thomas. "Ronald Reagan's Reformulation of the Rhetoric of War: Analysis of the 'Zero Option,' 'Evil Empire,' and 'Star Wars' Addresses." *Quarterly Journal of Speech,* no. 72 (1986): 390–414.

Graff, Gerald. *Clueless in Academe: How Schooling Obscures the Life of the Mind.* New Haven, CT: Yale University Press, 2004.

Gutmann, Amy, and Dennis Thompson. *Democracy and Disagreement.* Cambridge, MA: Belknap Press, 1996.

Habermas, Jürgen. *The Structural Transformation of the Public Sphere: An Inquiry into a Category of Bourgeois Society.* Cambridge, MA: MIT Press, 1991.

Halloran, Liz. "Obama's Notre Dame Visit Stirs Passions." National Public Radio, May 14, 2009. Available at http://www.npr.org/templates/story/story.php?storyId=104107546 (accessed March 25, 2010).

Hart, Roderick. *Seducing America: How Television Charms the Modern Voter.* Thousand Oaks, CA: Sage, 1998.

Heilemann, John, and Mark Halperin. *Game Change: Obama and the Clintons, McCain and Palin, and the Race of a Lifetime.* New York: Harper, 2010.

Herbst, Susan. *Numbered Voices: How Opinion Polling Has Shaped American Politics.* Chicago: University of Chicago Press, 1993.

———. *Politics at the Margin: Historical Studies of Public Opinion outside the Mainstream.* New York: Cambridge University Press, 1994.

———. "Public Opinion—Re-visited." *Breaux Symposium.* 2009.

Huffingtonpost.com. Sarah Palin RNC Convention Speech. September 3, 2008. Available at http://www.huffingtonpost.com/2008/09/03/sarah-palin-rnc-conventio_n_123703.html (accessed March 25, 2010).

Innis, Harold. *The Bias of Communication.* Toronto: University of Toronto Press, 2008.

International Debate Education Association. "About IDEA: Training Services." Available at http://www.idebate.org/about/training.php (accessed March 25, 2010).

Jamieson, Kathleen H. "Civility in the House of Representatives." *APPC Report* 10, March 1, 1997. Available at http://www.annenbergpublicpolicycenter.org/ NewsDetails.aspx?myId=195 (accessed March 25, 2010).

―――. "Civility in the House of Representatives: The 106th Congress." *Report Series: The Annenberg Public Policy Center of the University of Pennsylvania*. 2001.Available at http://www.annenbergpublicpolicycenter.org/Downloads/ Political_Communication/106thCongressCivil/2001_civility106th.pdf (accessed March 25, 2010).

―――. *Eloquence in an Electronic Age*. New York: Oxford University Press, 1988.

Jaschik, Scott. Tolerant Faculty, Intolerant Students. *Inside Higher Ed*, August 20, 2008. Available at http://www.insidehighered.com/news/2008/08/20/georgia (accessed March 25, 2010).

Jurkowitz, Mark. "Anger and Rancor Fuel Cable's Health Care Coverage." Journalism.org, August 2009. Available at http://www.journalism.org/index_ report/pej_news_coverage_index_august_1016_2009 (accessed March 25, 2010).

Kamiya, Gary. "The Dominatrix." Salon.com, September 9, 2008. Available at http://www.salon.com/opinion/kamiya/2008/09/09/mistress_palin/ (accessed March 25, 2010).

Kasson, John. *Rudeness and Civilization: Manners in Nineteenth-Century Urban America*. New York: Hill and Wang, 1990.

"Kathy Castor―Healthcare Town Hall Meeting in Tampa." YouTube, August 6, 2009. Available at http://www.youtube.com/watch?v=_kxaGfClPws (accessed March 25, 2010).

Kennedy, John. "Inaugural Address." American Presidency Project, January 20, 1961. Available at http://www.presidency.ucsb.edu/ws/index.php?pid= 8032&st (accessed March 25, 2010).

Kennedy, Randall. The Case against Civility. *American Prospect*, November 1, 1998. Available at http://www.prospect.org/cs/articles?article=the_case_ against_civility (accessed March 25, 2010).

Kettering Foundation. Available at http://www.kettering.org/ (accessed March 25, 2010).

Klein, James, and Julia Reichert. *Seeing Red*. VHS. 1983.

Lacks, Robyn, Jill Gordon, and Colleen McCue. "Who, What, and When: A Descriptive Examination of Crowd Formation, Crowd Behavior, and Participation with Law Enforcement at Homicide Scenes in One City." *American Journal of Criminal Justice*, no. 30 (2005): 1–20.

Landes, Joan B. *Women and the Public Sphere in the Age of the French Revolution.* Ithaca, NY: Cornell University Press, 1988.

Le Bon, Gustave. *The Crowd: A Study of the Popular Mind.* New York: Penguin, 1960.

Leibovich, Mark. "Among Rock-Ribbed Fans of Palin, Dudes Rule." *New York Times,* October 19, 2008, p. A1.

Lemann, Nicholas. "Conflict of Interests." *New Yorker,* August 11, 2008. Available at http://www.newyorker.com/arts/critics/atlarge/2008/08/11/080811crat_atlarge_lemann (accessed March 25, 2010).

Lin, Nan. *Social Capital: A Theory of Social Structure and Action.* Cambridge: Cambridge University Press, 2002.

Lipset, Seymour M., and Gary Marks. *It Didn't Happen Here: Why Socialism Failed in the United States.* New York: Norton, 2001.

Locke, John. *An Essay Concerning Human Understanding.* Alexander C. Fraser, ed. Oxford: Clarendon Press, 2007.

*Los Angeles Times.* Transcript: Obama's Notre Dame speech. May 17, 2009. Available at http://www.latimes.com/news/nationworld/nation/chi-barack-obama-notre-dame-speech,0,3194399,full.story (accessed March 25, 2010).

Love, Shawn M. "Online Debate: A Case Study Combining Traditional Strategy and Online Technology." 2004. Available at http://www.itdl.org/Journal/Sep_04/article06.htm (accessed March 25, 2010).

Macedo, Stephen, ed. *Deliberative Politics: Essays on Democracy and Disagreement.* New York: Oxford University Press, 1999.

MacGuffie, Bob. "Rocking the Town Halls—Best Practices." Right Principles. Available at http://thinkprogress.org/wp-content/uploads/2009/07/townhallactionmemo.pdf (accessed March 25, 2010).

Malkin, Michelle. "Massive Crowds, Missing MSM." September 10, 2008. Available at http://michellemalkin.com/2008/09/10/massive-crowds-missing-msm/ (accessed March 25, 2010).

Mason, Michael. "Flash: Barney Frank Gets Testy." *New York Times,* August 20, 2009. Available at http://prescriptions.blogs.nytimes.com/2009/08/20/news-flash-barney-frank-gets-testy/ (accessed March 25, 2010).

"McCain-Palin Mob in Strongsville, Ohio." Bloggerinterupted.com, October 8, 2008. Available at http://bloggerinterrupted.com/2008/10/video-the-mccain-palin-mob-in-strongsville-ohio (accessed March 25, 2010).

McCroskey, James, John Daly, and Gail Sorensen. "Personality Correlates of Communication Apprehension: A Research Note." *Human Communication Research* 3, no. 4 (2006): 376–380.

McDonald, Rachel. "Courteous Crowd Comes to Town Hall in Eugene." Oregon Public Radio, August 19, 2009. Available at http://news.opb.org/article/5654-courteous-crowd-comes-town-hall-eugene/ (accessed March 25, 2010).

McGerr, Michael. *The Decline of Popular Politics: The American North, 1865–1928.* New York: Oxford University Press, 1986.

McLuhan, Marshall. *Understanding Media.* New York: Signet, 1966.

Meehan, Eugene. "Civility as a Strategy in Litigation: Using It as a Tactical Tool." 2003. Available at http://www.supremecourtlaw.ca/default_e.asp?id=77 (accessed March 25, 2010).

Meyrowitz, Joshua. *No Sense of Place: The Impact of Electronic Media on Social Behavior.* New York: Oxford University Press, 1985.

Milbank, Dana. "In Fla., Palin Goes for the Rough Stuff as Audience Boos Obama." *Washington Post,* October 6, 2008. Available at http://voices.washingtonpost.com/44/2008/10/06/in_fla_palin_goes_for_the_roug.html (accessed March 25, 2010).

Mill, John Stuart. *On Liberty.* David Spitz, ed. New York: W. W. Norton, 1975.

Miller, Jonathan. "Worth Noting; Stop the Presses (or the Web Sites)." *New York Times,* March 12, 2006. Available at http://query.nytimes.com/gst/fullpage.html?res=990CE4DF1031F931A25750C0A9609C8B63 (accessed March 25, 2010).

Miller, Joshua R. "Critics Blast Obama's Scheduled Notre Dame Commencement Address." FoxNews.com, March 24, 2009. Available at http://www.foxnews.com/politics/first100days/2009/03/24/critics-blast-obamas-notre-dame-commencement-address/ (accessed March 25, 2010).

Montgomery, Lori, and Perry Bacon, Jr. "Key Senator Calls for Narrower Health Reform Measure: Republican Grassley Cites Town Hall Anger." *Washington Post,* August 20, 2009. Available at http://www.washingtonpost.com/wp-dyn/content/article/2009/08/19/AR2009081904125.html (accessed March 25, 2010).

Moore, Brooke Noel, and Richard Parker. *Critical Thinking.* New York: McGraw-Hill, 2008.

Mostrous, Alex. "White House Backs Right to Arms Outside Obama Events." *Washington Post,* August 19, 2009. Available at http://www.washingtonpost.com/wp-dyn/content/article/2009/08/18/AR2009081803416.html?hpid=topnews (accessed March 25, 2010).

Mutz, Diana. "Effects of 'In-Your-Face' Television Discourse on Perceptions of a Legitimate Opposition." *American Political Science Review,* 101, no. 4 (2007): 621–635).

Nardulli, Peter. *Domestic Perspectives on Contemporary Democracy.* Urbana, IL: University of Illinois Press, 2008.

Nathan, Rebekah. *My Freshman Year: What a Professor Learned by Becoming a Student.* Ithaca, NY: Cornell University Press, 2005.

Noelle-Neumann, Elisabeth. *The Spiral of Silence: Public Opinion—Our Social Skin.* Chicago: University of Chicago Press, 1984.

Nussbaum, E. Michael, and Gale Sinatra. "Argument and Conceptual Engagement." *Contemporary Educational Psychology*, no. 28 (2003): 384–395.

Otis, Ginger A. "'We Won't Pull Plug on Granny': O Rips Mercy-Kill 'Boogeymen' in Health Town Hall." *New York Post*, August 12, 2009. Available at http://www.nypost.com/seven/08122009/news/nationalnews/we_wont_pull_plug_on_granny_184093.htm (accessed March 25, 2010).

"Palin Misquotes Albright: Place in Hell Reserved for Women That Don't Support Other Women." Huffingtonpost.com, October 5, 2008. Available at http://www.huffingtonpost.com/2008/10/05/palin-misquotes-albright_n_131967.html (accessed March 25, 2010).

Papacharissi, Zizi. "Democracy Online: Civility, Politeness, and the Democratic Potential of Online Political Discussion Groups." *New Media and Society* 6, no. 2 (2004): 259–283.

Parsons, Talcott. "The School as a Social System." *Harvard Educational Review* 29 (1958): 297–318.

Peck, Dennis. "Civility: A Contemporary Context for a Meaningful Historical Concept." *Sociological Inquiry*, no. 72 (2002): 363–380.

Pew Forum on Religion and Public Life. "Obama, Catholics and the Notre Dame Commencement." April 30, 2009. Available at http://pewforum.org/Politics-and-Elections/Obama-Catholics-and-the-Notre-Dame-Commencement.aspx (accessed March 25, 2010).

Pew Research Center. "Better Ratings for Foreign Policy than Domestic Issues." April 23, 2009. Available at http://people-press.org/reports/pdf/509.pdf (accessed March 25, 2010).

———. "Internet Now Major Source of Campaign News: Continuing Partisan Divide in Cable TV News Audience." October 31, 2008. Available at http://people-press.org/report/467/internet-campaign-news (accessed March 25, 2010).

———. "Many Fault Media Coverage of Health Care Debate." August 6, 2009. Available at http://people-press.org/report/533/many-fault-media-coverage-of-health-care (accessed March 25, 2010).

Postman, Neil. *Amusing Ourselves to Death: Public Discourse in the Age of Show Business*. New York: Penguin, 1986.

Putnam, Robert. *Bowling Alone: The Collapse and Revival of American Community*. New York: Simon and Schuster, 2001.

———. "Robert Putnam Responds." *American Prospect* 25 (March–April 1996): 26–28. Available at http://www.prospect.org/cs/articles?article=unsolved_mysteries_the_tocqueville_files_311996_rp (accessed March 25, 2010).

Quirk, Paul. "When the President Speaks, How Do the People Respond?" *Critical Review*, no. 19 (2007): 427–446.

Recent presidential debate articles. Nielsenwire, October 21, 2008. Available at http://blog.nielsen.com/nielsenwire/tag/presidential-debate/ (accessed on March 25, 2010).

Rutten, Tim. "Incivility Is Taking the Place of Facts," *Denver Post*, September 25, 2009. Available at: http://www.denverpost.com/news/ci_13415748 (accessed March 25, 2010).

Ryan, Mary. *Women in Public: Between Banners and Ballots, 1825–1880*. Baltimore: Johns Hopkins University Press, 1992.

Sapiro, Virginia. "Considering Political Civility Historically: A Case Study of the United States" (paper presented at the Annual Meeting of the International Society for Political Psychology, 1999). Available at http://www.sam. kau.se/stv/ksspa/papers/sapiro_considering_political_civility_historically.pdf (accessed March 25, 2010).

"Sarah Palin: A Message to Alaskans about the Stimulus Veto and the Health Care Town Halls." Facebook. August 9, 2009. Available at http://www. facebook.com/note.php?note_id=114912353434 (accessed March 25, 2010).

"Sarah Palin: Statement on the Current Health Care Debate." Facebook. August 7, 2009. Available at http://www.facebook.com/note.php?note_id= 113851103434 (accessed March 25, 2010).

Seder, Andrew. "Secret Service Says 'Kill Him' Allegation Unfounded." *Times Leader*, October 17, 2008. Available at http://www.timesleader.com/news/ breakingnews/Secret_Service_says_Kill_him_allegation_unfounded_.html (accessed March 25, 2010).

Sinopoli, Richard. "Thick-Skinned Liberalism: Redefining Civility." *American Political Science Review* 89, no. 3 (1995): 614–615.

Smith, Adam C. "Protesters in Ybor City Drown Out Health Care Summit on Obama's Proposal." *St. Petersburg Times*, August 7, 2009. Available at http:// www.tampabay.com/news/politics/article1025529.ece (accessed March 25, 2010).

Sneed, Adam. "Obama Won't Receive ASU Honorary Degree." *State Press*, April 8, 2008. Available at http://www.statepress.com/node/5763 (accessed March 25, 2010).

StoryCorps. "About Us." Available at http://storycorps.org/about (accessed March 25, 2010).

Sullivan, Andrew. "Next Up: A CGI Palin." October 21, 2008. Available at http:// andrewsullivan.theatlantic.com/the_daily_dish/2008/10/palin-as-dean.html (accessed March 25, 2010).

Tarde, Gabriel. *New Encyclopedia International Journal of Criminology*, no. 2 (2005). Available at http://champpenal.revues.org/index.html (accessed March 25, 2010).

Tocqueville, Alexis de. *Democracy in America*. J. P. Mayer, ed. Garden City, NY: Anchor Books, 1969.

Tönnies, Ferdinand. *Community and Society*. Jose Harris, ed. Cambridge: Cambridge University Press, 2002.

Toulmin, Stephen. *The Uses of Argument*. Cambridge: Cambridge University Press, 1969.

Trygstad, Kyle, and Mike Momoli. "Before Friendly Crowd, Obama Urges Civility." Politics Nation, August 11, 2009. Available at http://www.realclearpolitics.com/politics_nation/2009/08/before_friendly_crowd_obama_ur.html (accessed March 25, 2010).

Tulis, Jeffrey. *The Rhetorical Presidency*. Princeton, NJ: Princeton University Press, 1987.

"2008 Year-End Google Zeitgeist." 2008. Google.com. Available at http://www.google.com/intl/en/press/zeitgeist2008/index.html (accessed March 25, 2010).

USNews.com. "Palin Speech Gets Rave Reviews." September 4, 2008. Available at http://www.usnews.com/usnews/politics/bulletin/bulletin_080904.htm (accessed March 25, 2010).

Vaughn, Lewis. *The Power of Critical Thinking: Effective Reasoning about Ordinary and Extraordinary Claims*. New York: Oxford University Press, 2007.

Walkowitz, Judith R. *City of Dreadful Delight: Narratives of Sexual Danger in Late-Victorian London*. Chicago: University of Chicago, 1992.

*Wall Street Journal*. Transcript of Palin's Announcement. July 3, 2009. Available at http://blogs.wsj.com/washwire/2009/07/03/transcript-of-palins-announcement/ (accessed March 25, 2010).

White, James B. *When Words Lose Their Meaning: Constitutions and Reconstitutions of Language, Character, and Community*. Chicago: University of Chicago Press, 1985.

Wilentz, Sean. "Who Lincoln Was." *New Republic*, July 15, 2009.

Williams, Raymond. *Television: Technology and Cultural Form*. London: Routledge, 2003.

Winner, Langdon. *Autonomous Technology: Technics-Out-of-Control as a Theme in Political Thought*. Cambridge, MA: MIT Press, 1977.

Wolf, Naomi. *The Beauty Myth: How Images of Beauty Are Used Against Women*. New York: Anchor, 1992.

Zarefsky, David. "Presidential Rhetoric and the Power of Definition." *Presidential Studies Quarterly*, no. 34 (2004): 612–613.

Zittrain, Jonathan. *The Future of the Internet—And How to Stop It*. New Haven, CT: Yale University Press, 2009.

# Index

take their advertising at face value—hopes to achieve the highest-quality public communication about politics as "the best news team on television," they would do well to innovate and try to influence Internet dialogue among their valued viewers and readers. They have the floor, and they have our attention.

## Influencing the Future of Civility: Listening

Better articulating one's claim and engaging in debate is one step in the pursuit of civility. But hearing these arguments and taking them seriously, engaging in "hard listening," is equally important. Listening to in-person argumentation demands a certain level of etiquette, regardless of whether the conversation ends up constructively. Certainly in a classroom or town meeting there are norms for behavior: It is generally unacceptable to interrupt too often, to fall asleep, or to leave in disgust.

The world of mediated and online argumentation is another story altogether. If political Web site editors engage in the structured argumentation discussed in the previous section, they can dismiss arguments and evidence that reveal a lack of listening: If someone has not read or processed the previous remarks or instructions, their contributions can be rejected. But can we get past these mechanics and think more broadly about how to become a better culture of listeners?

While "hard listening" in policy debate seems an attractive path to pursue, not many in the journalistic community have worked to achieve the goal of better listening. There are a variety of talk program hosts who fail or succeed with on-air callers, although the failures seem far more pervasive than the successes. Many ideological hosts are seeking to maintain high ratings and keep their advertising revenue flowing, a purpose that demands playing to the bulk of listeners. As partisan radio hosts well know, like-minded people seek them out for entertainment and reinforcement of their views, so they need to deliver what the audience came for. This rational attempt to read these strings of comments, and find them intriguing.[25] But it is unlikely that any citizen or policy maker would gain much from them with regard to the sort of argumentation needed to create better public policy.

What might a managed discussion look like, on a site like the CNN *Ticker*? An editor or journalist, with some brief training in argumentation, could transform this string of comments into a coherent discussion without much difficulty, although it would take an investment of funds and effort on the part of the network. A journalist, moderating this discussion, could simply push contributors a bit, demanding clarification, evidence, and logic: "What do you mean by that? What is your evidence? Did you see our program yesterday on this subject, where we present an opposing view?" If this sounds pedagogical—asking a CNN moderator to *teach* participants how to argue—it is. While the supportive teacher-type voice is often missing in American journalism these days, most good reporters and editors still see themselves as supportive of a productive public discourse. Argumentation training would enable a moderator of the CNN *Ticker* to guide the tenor of the discussion, just as it does with beginning high school debaters, making it more interesting and more intelligent. If this is done well, regular contributors would start demanding clarification and evidence from each other, as students do in a class, after a teacher shows them what is expected.

Again, regulation of argument—setting up a structure, either Toulminesque or using another format—and asking that people post *within that structure* takes a commitment of time, money, and thought.[26] An editor or editors would be necessary, and there is a risk that fewer people would write in. This may be a short-term price to pay, with regard to size of audience involvement (CNN, like any profit-oriented news organization, wants maximum participation). But the quality of discourse would be heightened, and quickly. A powerful network, with a tiny investment, might actually make a difference, aiding in the creation of a national argument culture. A variety of sites can pursue this, of course. But if CNN—and we shall